MW01283170

WORLD
202.
What is Our Future?
Cycles of Transformation in Vedic Astrology

Learn Vedic Astrology at: www.universityofvedicastrology.com
Contact Joni Patry at: www.galacticcenter.org

Copyright 2024 by Joni Patry

All rights reserved. No part of this book may be reproduced, stored in a database or other retrieval system, or transmitted in any form, by any means, including mechanical, electronic, photocopy, recording, or otherwise, without prior written permission of the publisher.

Published by Madeline Zech Ruiz

ISBN: 978-1-952114-65-6

Book cover design and typesetting by Aleksandar Petrovic — vajsman@gmail.com

Copyright Number TX 9-313-188

JONI PATRY

WORLD PREDICTIONS
2024 to 2042

What is Our Future?
Cycles of Transformation
in Vedic Astrology

Contents

Dedication

As a child I saw psychic astrologer Jeane Dixon on television the day before President Kennedy came to Dallas beg him not to go to Dallas because she feared an assassination. I never forgot her prediction and I always wondered if he had listened to her could this horrible event been prevented. This was the beginning of my search to understand Astrology to learn the power of prediction.

Throughout my 45 years of study, I discovered the power of the lunar nodes Rahu and Ketu which create the eclipses as they come together with the three outer planets (Uranus, Neptune and Pluto), Saturn, Jupiter and specifically the signs and nakshatras they transited in. These transiting planets are what predict major events globally.

Astrology is my life's purpose, and I know it is the Divine science that can help give us guidance as a humanity to raise consciousness. It can be used to transform and change the world. It is my mission to make Vedic astrology mainstream.

I began the University of Vedic Astrology in 2016 to teach others the power of astrology and how through prediction we can change the course of life and follow our Divine path. My students have given me the inspiration to stay on my path.

My most dedicated and original student of all is Shreekala Ram, affectionately known to everyone as Shree. She is totally committed and helped me with everything. She is just as passionate as I am for the art and science of Vedic Astrology. Our quest is to educate and enlighten the world to the value and purpose of astrology. We both feel the passion of this mission. She has helped and inspired me to write this book. She was instrumental in finding certain time frames for events through her invaluable research. She is genuine and is the essence of a truly spiritual soul and a loyal friend. I could not have run the University without her. She has helped me in so many ways, I am eternally grateful. I am blessed to have her in my life. I am so proud of her, she has become a brilliant astrologer.

I am truly blessed to have such loyal and loving friends. Juliana Swanson is always generously unconditionally offering information from her vast knowledge and research. She is an amazing astrologer with no ego and a true friend. I always respect her information as she is sincere in all she does.

Madeline Zech Ruiz has helped in me with her great talent and intelligence. She mastered the science of astrology in record time and has inspired me through her expertise in both business and technology. She is truly brilliant! She is also a great teacher inspiring the new students as a tutor. But most of all she is instrumental in publishing my books. This book could not be what it is without her.

My three sons Christian, Preston and Austin are my greatest accomplishment in this life! They are incredible in their own ways, but my youngest son Austin has been instrumental with my astrology business and helps me in every way to fulfill my mission to make Vedic Astrology mainstream. He helped me make my YouTube channel, social media, website, and is the inspiration for my Galactic Planner which is the tool that everyone can use to utilize astrology every day. It calculates your personal transits and what they indicate daily, and it is delivered to your calendar on your phone or computer. This is how everyone can use astrology for guidance. This makes astrology usable for everyone.

I want to thank my three sons for always believing in me and especially my husband Daniel who has always believed in me and my astrology ever since we met in high school. I could not be who I am and accomplish my mission without the support of my family and friends.

Introduction

The origins of this book began from my quest to better understand prediction, in how the cycles of the planets have always been in effect, especially in terms of world events. Throughout my life as I've studied astrology, I have always found that the nodes of the Moon, Rahu and Ketu, were the most powerful and meaningful connectors in the heavens and have made their mark on the world.

As I contemplated the meanings of Rahu and Ketu, I came to discover that they are the connectors of the Sun, the Moon, and the Earth. These arbitrary points in space are simply where the Sun, the Moon, and the Earth come together. Rahu is the point in space where the Moon crosses the ecliptic going upward, (ascending) whereas Ketu is where the Moon crosses the ecliptic going downward (descending). The ecliptic is the path of the Sun as it revolves around the Earth. Eclipses occur when the Sun, Earth and Moon align, therefore this is when Rahu and Ketu come together with the new Moon (solar eclipse), and the full Moon (lunar eclipse), eclipses occur twice a year six months apart.

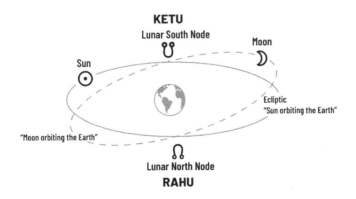

The next important variable in studying astrology is the deep understanding of the power of Jupiter and Saturn. These two planets are called the social planets as they pertain to earthly matters particularly when dealing with the economy and society. These planets have vast implications concerning societal matters, governmental matters as well as our own personal financial matters. They form a conjunction every 20 years and alternately form an opposition in half that time 10 years later. When Jupiter and Saturn form a conjunction, they usually have a profound effect in a positive way on the economy globally.

One of the most important variables in studying long range world predictions are the three outer planets, Uranus, Neptune, and Pluto. Since they stay in signs for longer durations they have profound effects on world affairs. Their stay in certain signs will form different generations of people which have different needs, likes, and purposes. The outer planets are transpersonal ruling the collective unconscious, they affect world consciousness as a whole and direct the many changes in society, and cultural differences throughout the world. They affect the evolution of our mind in consciousness therefore growth of awareness through humanity. In other words, what the whole of humanity comprehend.

Rahu and Ketu are a nodal axis, exactly opposite and transit through the signs always opposing each other. As they align with the outer planets and Saturn and Jupiter, they create the biggest, most transformational changes of all. In this book you will better understand how looking historically at the past lineups of this nodal axis and aligning with the three outer planets combined with Jupiter or Saturn, humanity goes through abrupt chaotic, catastrophic changes. With these lineups, we can predict global events that have changed the world forever.

The next variable used to understand the flavor of the events is to look at what signs Rahu and Ketu are in. These signs can indicate the kind of events to be occurring especially when the lunar nodes go into Gemini and Sagittarius. There are other signs that are quite disruptive and extreme but the most severe and catastrophic from my research equates to events occurring when Rahu is in Gemini and Ketu is in Sagittarius. I came upon this realization after the tragedy of September 11, 2001, when terrorists destroyed the World Trade centers in New York. I started to notice that during this time Rahu was conjunct Jupiter and Ketu was conjunct Mars. These planets were the triggers that activated not only Rahu and Ketu but the monumental devastation that occurs when they are in these signs. I then began looking back to the previous time when Rahu was in Gemini and Ketu was in Sagittarius and discovered it was 1982. This was a time of great fear with the AIDS virus. I Then began to look back at the last time Rahu was in Gemini and Ketu was in Sagittarius 18 1/2 years prior to that, which was when John F. Kennedy was assassinated in 1963. Taking it back another 18 1/2 years I came to discover this was in 1945 which was the bombing of Hiroshima.

It was when I began writing my book in 2017 "Rahu and Ketu our Karmic Destiny"

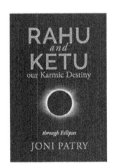

that I discovered Rahu would be transiting into Gemini and Ketu in Sagittarius again in 2019 -2020. January through February of 2020 Mars would be the trigger that activated this nodal axis, and I predicted in my book in 2017 that 2020 would have a catastrophic event that would change the world forever. Sadly, as I predicted in advance the COVID-19 virus came upon the world at that time and changed the world forever.

The main reason I wanted to write this book was because I wanted to look forward to the next time that Rahu would be in Gemini and Ketu in Sagittarius. This will occur in the year of 2037 – 2038. It appears to me that this combination looks even more severe than the ones before. It is my intention to have this book in print, so people have the opportunity to understand the power of prediction with Vedic astrology and prepare for the next catastrophic event.

During these years specifically in May of 2038 there will be a devastating lineup of Rahu in Sagittarius with Mars, Jupiter, and Uranus. Mars is the trigger that activates events while Jupiter expands them, and Uranus is the wild card that will make it an unexpected, sudden, and extremely violent event.

It is very important that we understand what signs the nodal axis of Rahu and Ketu are in and give them more depth and meaning for our daily lives. We must look to the nakshatras that they are in as well. There are 12 signs of the zodiac each 30° segments of the 360-degree zodiac. Nakshatras used in Vedic astrology are smaller portions of the Zodiac with divisions of 13 ° 20 minutes. There are 27 of these segments and their meanings are derived from the stars in these portions of the Zodiac. Certain nakshatras are more dangerous and devastating so they flavor the meanings of all the planets, as well as Rahu and Ketu. Lastly, within these nakshatras the stars that give the nakshatras their meanings have powerful and specific effects. If the eclipses, outer planets Uranus, Neptune, and Pluto or Saturn and Jupiter are conjunct one of the fixed stars within a few degrees, they will add meaning to the events based on what these fixed stars are known to produce and indicate.

In this book I have gone through all 12 signs that Rahu and Ketu transit remembering that Rahu and Ketu are always exactly opposite therefore the two opposing signs that they are in will be activated such as Aries/ Libra, Taurus/Scorpio, Gemini/Sagittarius, Cancer/Capricorn, Leo/ Aquarius, and Virgo/Pisces.

I have taken a look back historically as to what they have produced in the past with major events, world catastrophes, and then a look at the combinations for each of the consecutive years to come starting from the year 2024 through the year of 2042. Within this time frame Rahu and Ketu will go through all 12 signs of the Zodiac. Actually they change signs every 18 months – Year and a half. They do take 18 ½ years to go through all 12 signs but they are in one sign for 18 months.

One last note, as I was processing all the planets relative to the nodal axis with Uranus, Neptune, and Pluto, and tying them in together with Saturn and Jupiter, I discovered another very treacherous time in the future 2030-2031. Specifically, May and June of 2030. There is a lineup of planets that absolutely represent shocking and explosive events.

In the year of 2030 Saturn is conjunct Ketu and Uranus in Taurus opposing Jupiter and Rahu in Scorpio. The last time that Saturn aligned with Uranus and Ketu was the beginning of World War II, except during that time they were in Aries, and Saturn was debilitated in Aries, so it was far worse. During this time of 2030 Jupiter is magnified by being in Scorpio with Rahu. This will prove to be a very difficult time as there are stars that are very dangerous in Scorpio and Taurus, which are Antares and Aldebaran. These stars create war and conflict.

My sincere desire for writing this book is to help people understand and use the most Divine Science of all, which is astrology. Astrology can give us guidance, understanding, and wisdom through the ages for our Earthly evolution as one humanity and consciousness.

CHAPTER 1

Cycles that Transform the World

Global Predictions for the next 18 Years

The focus of this book is the 18½ year cycle of the Moon's nodes through all the signs and nakshatras with a focus on the power of Eclipses in these signs.

Rahu and Ketu are exactly opposite and stay in a sign for 18 ½ months. Since there are 12 signs of the Zodiac it takes 18 1/2 years for Rahu and Ketu to transit through all 12 signs of the Zodiac.

This book is structured to give an understanding of Rahu and Ketu in the zodiacal signs, nakshatras, conjunct planets, and fixed stars.

The Zodiac is 360° and is divided up by the 12 signs of the Zodiac each extending for 30° segments. On another level there are 27 nakshatras each extending for segments of 13° 20 minutes. As Rahu and Ketu and all the planets in our solar system transit through the Zodiac they are transiting through the signs and the nakshatras. The signs and the nakshatras flavor the meanings of Rahu and Ketu and the planets. This has a profound effect on global affairs and our lives.

What are the Moon's nodes – Rahu and Ketu?

The Moon's nodes map the points in the zodiac where the Moon crosses the ecliptic, the apparent plane in which Earth revolves around the Sun. At the time of eclipses, the Moon is also aligned in the same plane, allowing it to obscure the Sun, or Earth's shadow to obscure the Moon.

The points where the Moon crosses the ecliptic are constantly moving. This movement is always relative to the motion of the Sun and Moon as seen from Earth. These points in space are symbolic of Earth's interaction within our limited cosmos, the solar system. This is all about our earthly experiences, the duality of the Sun and Moon engaging with the third element, Earth.

The Moon's orbit around Earth intersects the ecliptic at two points. These two points are called the nodes of the Moon. The north node of the Moon (Rahu) is the ascending node where the Moon crosses from the southern to the northern hemisphere. This symbolizes birth, an entrance into material manifestation. The south node (Ketu) is the descending node where the Moon crosses from the northern to the southern hemisphere, symbolically an exit from the material world and into the spiritual realm. So, Rahu takes us into the physical world and Ketu takes us out of it.

The Sun and Moon symbolize the father and mother who give birth to this world. They are integral to the symbolism of our experience here on Earth.

In the Hindu myth of Rahu and Ketu, a serpent slithered between the Sun and Moon to partake of the nectar of immortality that was being given to the gods, who are symbolized by the planets and luminaries. When the thief was discovered, Lord Vishnu threw a disk, splitting him in half, but he'd already swallowed the nectar of immortality. This division severed the serpent's head (Rahu) from the serpent's tail (Ketu). The fact that it had come between the Sun and Moon alludes to the fact that this point causes eclipses. Rahu and Ketu are referred to as shadow planets. The shadows cast imply a universal truth – that which cannot be seen or understood constitutes a mystery of life. Our conscious awareness is blocked as we enter this worldly dimension. We are cast into darkness and emerge as life on Earth, influenced ever after by the Sun and Moon, whose symbolism is woven into our unconsciousness.

As we are born into this world the awareness of the other realms from which we've come are forgotten, blanked out of our minds. We're suddenly separated from our past, and now beginning the process of learning through the thinking mind.

Rahu represents the head consumed with the thinking mind. But the mind separated from spirit creates illusions, and Rahu is the indicator of worldly illusions. Ketu is the quality of knowing without thinking. It is the spiritual connection that can give insights that lead to enlightenment. Rahu is the materialistic physical world, and Ketu is the spiritual world that is beyond this earthly domain. But we still carry Ketu's essence within us, and that's what connects us to the eternal world beyond.

All this represents the cycles of birth and death into and out of this world. Rahu and Ketu are the indicators of destiny and fate, symbolizing our entrapment in this physical plane. These shadow planets control us by our desires. Our desires are our karmas. Our destiny is to release the chains this world has cast upon us. It is like the serpent's bite. The poisonous venom intoxicates us with the desire for worldly experience. Rahu takes us under its spell with the illusions of this world, the promise of happiness: "If I could only have more of the things that give me pleasure." But of course, this only leads to insatiable desires. We can never have enough. And since nothing in this world is lasting, desire will always cause us suffering. This is the venomous bite of Rahu.

Conversely, Ketu strips us of the objects of our desires, revealing that nothing in this world gives us security and permanence. It is essentially the process of enlightenment, when we come to realize that, ultimately, it's all an illusion. Nothing of this material world lasts; it's all Maya, a delusion. Ketu is the bringer of enlightenment through the realization of this truth. Ketu is the release of this world. Just as Rahu is our entrapment, Ketu is our final liberation from the karmas of the soul. Whereas Rahu will give things for a price, Ketu will take things away but leave enlightenment in its place.

Human beings spend most of their time in their minds. Although we exist in this world, we're often not part of it because we separate ourselves in our minds. Our eternal nature is Unity and, when not a part of this earthly experience (within the entrapment of Rahu and Ketu), we are one with everything. This is a hard concept to imagine on Earth because all we know are endings, beginnings, and separations from each other. That sense of separation comes from the mind. As the head of the serpent, Rahu represents the mind. Our most natural state is to be one with all. To be separate is unnatural. When we're one with all, we feel complete and whole without fear. This is our natural state when in spirit. Rahu can represent fear because it essentially blocks out reality and keeps us trapped in the illusion of this world, separating us from truth or the Divine source that connects us with everything. The knowledge and truth of who we are beyond this world of separation is contained in the meaning of Ketu. Ketu gives us glimpses beyond this world, but we can't really conceive of it due to the limitations of our mind, which is a part of the illusion.

An understanding of Rahu and Ketu can lend insight into the meaning of eclipses. Eclipses offer us glimpses of what lies beyond this world. When eclipses occur there's an opportunity to see the truth during the brief unveiling of the illusion. When the illusion is swept aside during an eclipse, these are times that allow a vision beyond this world. This means that which controls our earthly experience of the world (Sun/Moon) is blocked and we can see beyond it. Even the pattern of day and night is obliterated because a solar eclipse can introduce the darkness of night in the middle of the day.

In ancient times people didn't understand what was happening and believed it was the end of the world. For a few minutes at least, it certainly would have felt like that. This radical disruption of a normal day would inevitably have provoked some sort of psychological "time out." Hence, to this day, there's still a sort of primal fear that persists around the times of solar eclipses.

A solar eclipse is when the Sun's light is blocked by the Moon, throwing Earth into a brief period of darkness during the day. Symbolically, we might say that what has been awakened in the dark will be revealed. Even the casual observer will often notice there are more tragedies and upsets around the time of a solar eclipse. I hear sirens more often during the two-week period between the solar and the lunar eclipse.

Solar eclipses occur at the time of the New Moon, meaning something new is being presented out of the darkness, something will be revealed. Two weeks later, that which has been revealed will come to light when the Moon is full. Lunar eclipses occur when Earth's shadow blocks the sunlight that would normally reflect off the Moon. In our emotional darkness the truth may seem obscured, but our shadows will be revealed. Most of us can't bear to see the dark side of our nature, so denial usually sets in. The shadow aspect of our nature prevents us from realizing our spiritual truth.

The Solar eclipse is the point of focus as there may be a lunar eclipse two weeks before or after the solar eclipse or there may not even be a lunar eclipse. Eclipses are determined by the New Moon (solar eclipse) or full Moon (lunar eclipse) closeness to the nodes (Rahu and Ketu). The lunar eclipse is an offshoot of the solar eclipse.

In Jungian psychology the "shadow" refers to an unconscious aspect of the personality which constitutes the ego. It is our dark side that is hidden in our subconscious mind. It is our instinctual nature that we are taught to suppress as children as we are taught morals. Understanding the shadow side can alleviate unconscious behaviors of projection in ourselves and others.

In essence, eclipses bring us the opportunity to see whatever in our being is preventing us from the most important thing we're here to realize – to grow spiritually and transcend the illusion of this world. This process will reveal all of our weaknesses and fears. Fear is a manifestation of this world (Rahu) because while in this world we're entrapped in its illusions. Ultimately, we must come to the realization that this world is only a false perception of reality.

Rahu is the entrance into this illusionary world and Ketu is our exit to a spiritual world that holds imaginary powers while in the physical world. Therefore, Rahu indicates our future and what we are here to discover through this lifetime while Ketu is our gifts from the past and can determine what we brought with us in terms of our realizations of our good and bad karma. Together they direct our life in the here and now as the future prospects unite with the learning of the past to create our destiny in life.

Eclipses are the most powerful tool for prediction that we have as astrologers. As Rahu and Ketu transit through the signs, nakshatras, and with the planets and stars, many future predictions can be indicated by understanding their past cycles and results. This gives the power to make future predictions.

The signs that Rahu and Ketu reside in for 18 months are the signs that the eclipses will occur. Therefore, if Rahu or Ketu are conjunct with other planets at the time of an eclipse, they will stimulate world events relative to what that planet represents. Planets conjunct an eclipse is engulfed in darkness and the shadow side of that planet is revealed. This brings to light something to be healed. For example, when the eclipses conjunct Jupiter it influences the economy since Jupiter signifies wealth.

Planets conjunct Rahu and Ketu at the time of eclipses will see their effects magnified. The aspect to Jupiter and Saturn affects financial and social affairs. Similarly, the aspects of Rahu and Ketu upon the outer planets, Uranus, Neptune, and Pluto are transpersonal provoking world changes, consistent with their nature. Mars is always a trigger for events and is conditioned by the sign it occupies when aspecting the nodes. The inferior planets (Mercury and Venus), with the nodes, also exert an influence at the time of an eclipse.

Transiting Rahu and Ketu stay in a sign for 18 months. There are two eclipses a year, six months apart occurring in opposing signs. The eclipses generally occur within 12°-18° of the positions of Rahu and Ketu. The sign they are in will determine the results of those eclipses but there are other details that give the Rahu/Ketu transit very specific results, particularly at the time of the eclipses.

Here are the factors that influence the results according to their placements:

1) Sign and nakshatra placement of Rahu and Ketu (eclipses)
2) Planets conjunct and opposed Rahu and Ketu (eclipses)
3) Fixed stars conjunct Rahu and Ketu (eclipses)

Planets conjunct an eclipse will lend their indications and meanings through the events produced. Slower-moving planets influence eclipses because they are in the sign with the nodes for a longer period. Saturn and Jupiter influence the nodes, especially in financial matters. Saturn is treacherous and Jupiter can expand and magnify dangerous effects. The outer planets Uranus, Neptune, and Pluto can cause extremes according to their nature. Uranus indicates sudden unexpected events, Neptune indicates deception and delusions, and Pluto brings power struggles. Mars is a trigger when it aspects Rahu and Ketu, activating events at the time of aspect, generally provoking violence.

The signs of Rahu and Ketu will flavor the experience according to their nature and meanings. The nakshatras give specific meanings, typically in accordance with the meaning of fixed stars in this portion of the zodiac. If an eclipse is conjunct a fixed star it will give the results of that star.

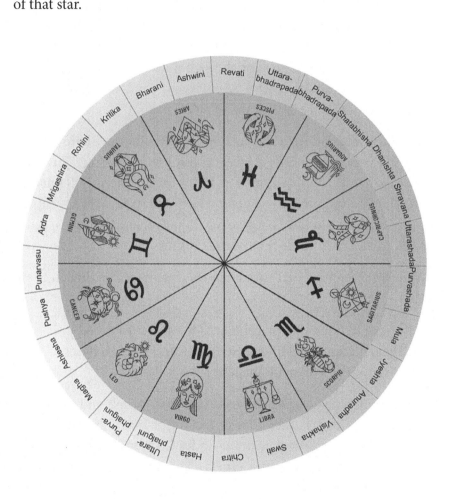

Table1: Zodiacal wheel placements of Nakshatras

The 28 Nakshatras

	Nakshatra	Ruler	Degrees of Zodiac	Degrees in Sign
1	**Ashwini**	Ketu	0°00' to 13°20'	0°00' to 13°20' Aries
2	**Bharani**	Venus	13°20' to 26°40'	13°20' to 26°40' Aries
3	**Krittika**	Sun	26°40' to 40°00'	26°40' Aries to 10°00' Taurus
4	**Rohini**	Moon	40°00' to 53°20'	10°00' to 23°20' Taurus
5	**Mrigasira**	Mars	53°20' to 66°40'	23°20' Taurus to 6°40' Gemini
6	**Ardra**	Rahu	66°40' to 80°00'	6°40' to 20°00' Gemini
7	**Punarvasu**	Jupiter	80°00 to 93°20'	20°00' Gemini to 3°20' Cancer
8	**Pushya**	Saturn	93°20' to 106°40'	3°20' to 16°20' Cancer
9	**Ashlesha**	Mercury	106°40' to 120°00'	16°40' Cancer to 0°00' Leo
10	**Magha**	Ketu	120°00' to 133°20'	0°00' to 13°20' Leo
11	**P Phalguni**	Venus	133°20' to 146°40'	13°20' to 26°40' Leo
12	**U Phalguni**	Sun	146°40' to 160°00'	26°40' Leo to 10°00' Virgo
13	**Hasta**	Moon	160°00' to 173°20'	10°00' to 23°20' Virgo
14	**Chitra**	Mars	173°20' to 186°40'	23°20' Virgo to 6°40' Libra
15	**Swati**	Rahu	186°40' to 200°00'	6°40' to 20°00' Libra
16	**Vishakha**	Jupiter	200°00' to 213°20'	20°00' Libra to 3°20' Scorpio
17	**Anuradha**	Saturn	213°20' to 226°40'	3°20' to 16°40' Scorpio
18	**Jyeshta**	Mercury	226°40' to 240°00'	16°40' Scorpio to 0°00' Sagittarius
19	**Mula**	Ketu	240°00' to 253°20'	0°00' to 13°20' Sagittarius
20	**P Ashadha**	Venus	253°20' to 266°40'	13°20' to 26°40' Sagittarius
21	**U Ashadha**	Sun	266°40' to 280°00'	26°40' Sag to 10°00' Capricorn
22	**Abhijit**		276°40' to 280°53'20"	6°40' to 10 °53'20' Capricorn
23	**Shravana**	Moon	280°00' to 293°20'	10°00' to 23°20' Capricorn
24	**Dhanishta**	Mars	293°20' to 306°40'	23°20' Cap to 6°40' Aquarius
25	**Shatabhishak**	Rahu	306°40' to 320°00'	6°40' to 20°00' Aquarius
26	**Purva Bhadra**	Jupiter	320°00' to 333°20'	20°00' Aquarius to 3°20' Pisces
27	**Uttara Bhadra**	Saturn.	333°20' to 346°40'	3°20' to 16°40' Pisces
28	**Revati**	Mercury	346°40' to 360°00'	16°40' to 30°00' Pisces

Table 2: Zodiacal placements of Nakshatras

Future Predictions 2024 - 2042

In the following chapters we will look at all future predictions for the years 2024-2042 based on the position of the nodes Rahu and Ketu. For reference here are the positions

Fixed Stars

Fixed Star	Description	Western Position	Vedic Position
El Sheratan	'the two signs'. This star represents danger when acting impulsively	3 58 Taurus	10.07 Anes
Almach	cheerful nature likes change and variety. Popularity brings benefit from others	14.14 Taurus	20.23 Anes
Menkar	associated with disgrace and loss of fortune	14.19 Taurus	20.28 Anes
Alcyone - The Weeping Sisters	brightest star of sorrow and also star of success ana prominence	0 00 Gemini	6.09 Taurus
Algol - The Weeping Sisters	demon most violent and evil of stars Deals with losing one's head, figuratively and literally	26 10 Taurus	2.19 Taurus
Aldebaran -The Weeping Sisters	honor, intelligence. extraordinary energy and enthusiasm, tut threat of danger from enemies	9.47 Gemini	15.56 Taurus
Betelgeuse	martial honor, power, and wealth	28.45 Gemini	4.54 Gemini
Sirius	considered royal one, but also quite violent, gives honor beyond grave, famous dean	14 05 Cancer	20.14 Gemini
Castor - Gemini Twin	the mortal twin, known for his sharp intellect, fame and honor with loss of fortune	20.14 Cancer	26.23 Gemini
Pollux - Gemini Twin	immortal twin, known for finning stalls known for courage and ruthlessness	23.13 Cancer	29.22 Gemini
Acubens	nurturing and preserving, but nervous nature. Good for affairs with public	13.39 Leo	19.48 Cancer

Fixed Star	Description	Western Position	Vedic Position
Regulus	royal fixed star noted tor kings and leaders, great tame and quest for power	29.50 Leo	5.59 Leo
Aglenubi (shows as Denebola)	gives creative, artistic abilities	21.37 Virgo	27.46 Leo
Zosma	star of egotism and self-indulgence	11.19 Virgo	17.28 Leo
Algorab	star of hindrances, success in business but eventual fals	13.27 Libra	19.36 Virgo
Spica	one of the most auspicious stars of all denoting success, fame, honors, wealth, and a love of the arts and sciences	23.50 Libra	29.59 Virgo
Acturus	gives riches, renown prosperity and success in fine arts	24.14 Libra	.23 Libra
Antares	high intelligence, honors and power, but with sudden loss. Political and Miliary star	9 46 Libra	15.55 Scorpio
Kaus Borealis	associated with idealistic, altruist-: qualities, and a strong need for justice	6 19 Capricorn	12.28 Sagittarius
The Galactic Center	where cosmic intelligence originates. Center of the galaxy	26 Sagittarius	2.09 Sagittarius
Altair	gives a bold, bright, ambitious nature. It leads to positions of power, but trouble with authority	1.47 Aquarius	7.56 Capricorn
Formalhaut	can be very treacherous or very benefic. Possesses creativity, especially musical talent	3.52 Pisces	10.01 Aquarius
Markab	headstrong nature. Fated star of sorrow	23.28 Pisces	29.37 Aquarius
Scheat	star of literary and poetic ability, but also implies extreme loss and sorrow	29.22 Pisces	5.31 Pisces

Table 3: Fixed Stars

Rahu and Ketu through the 12 signs of the zodiac 2024 -2042

November 28, 2023 – May 29, 2025	Rahu in Pisces / Ketu in Virgo
May 29, 2025 – November 25, 2026	Rahu in Aquarius / Ketu in Leo
November 25, 2026 – May 24, 2028	Rahu in Capricorn / Ketu in Cancer
May 24, 2028 – February 04, 2030	Rahu in Sagittarius / Ketu in Gemini
February 04, 2030 – August 09, 2031	Rahu in Scorpio / Ketu in Taurus
August 09, 2031 – January 29, 2033	Rahu in Libra / Ketu in Aries
January 29, 2033 – August 12, 2034	Rahu in Virgo / Ketu in Pisces
August 12, 2034 – April 12, 2036	Rahu in Leo / Ketu in Aquarius
April 12, 2036 – October 19, 2037	Rahu in Cancer / Ketu in Capricorn
October 19, 2037 – April 07 2039	Rahu in Gemini / Ketu in Sagittarius
April 07, 2039 – December 12, 2040	Rahu in Taurus / Ketu in Scorpio
December 12, 2040 – June 21, 2042	Rahu in Aries / Ketu in Libra
June 21, 2042 - December 19, 2043	Rahu in Pisces / Ketu in Virgo

CHAPTER 2

Rahu in Pisces and Ketu in Virgo

November 28, 2023 to May 29, 2025

Looking back at previous times when the lunar nodes were in these signs we see some devastating times particularly around assassinations. Interestingly, in July 2024 there was a serious assassination attempt on President Trump as he was running for re-election.

There were major storms and hurricanes such as Hurricane Katrina and crisis in the ocean such as when the Titanic sunk. It was even a time of disease because Virgo is a sign of health and disease.

Nakshatras Activated

Rahu in Pisces (Purva Bhadrapada, Uttara Bhadrapada, Revati) and Ketu in Virgo (Uttara Phalguni, Hasta, Chitra).

What happened before:

Rahu was in Pisces, Ketu in Virgo in 1968 when Martin Luther King Jr and Robert (Bobby) Kennedy were assassinated. Also during this time was the largest loss of life of American soldiers in the Vietnam War. With corruption at its peak in many governments, this was the time of rebellion when youth around the world were fighting back.

Saturn was with Rahu during the King and Kennedy assassinations, with devastating results for the civil rights movement. When Saturn and Rahu conjoin by transit, there seems to be overwhelming and sad events. Saturn was with Rahu (in Libra) when President Lincoln was assassinated, and together in Gemini when the atomic bomb was dropped on Hiroshima.

Rahu was in the last degrees of Pisces when the Titanic sank April 15th, 1912. The last degrees of a water sign are *gandanta* which means drowning. Over 1500 people lost their lives in this tragedy.

Hurricane Katrina hit New Orleans on August 29, 2005. Ketu was tightly conjoined Jupiter in Virgo. When Rahu is in Pisces, it seems the waters rise and cause destruction, while Jupiter's involvement magnifies the potential.

7th h. 21	8th h. 24	9th h. 27	10th h. 30
♄ 25:18 Rev ♃ 23:36 Rev ♂ 21:55 Rev ☿ 03:07 PBh ♀ 01:46 PBh	♂ 12:28 Ash	☽ 09:00 Ard	
6th h. 26	Martin Luther King Jr Assassination		11th h. 34
	Thu 04-04-1968		
	18:01:00		
	Memphis, Tennessee		
5th h. 40	USA		12th h. 27
	Timezone: 6 DST: 0		
	Latitude: 35N08'58	♃℞ 02:51 Mag	
	Longitude: 90W02'56	♀℞ 27:30 UPh	
	Ayanamsha : -23:24:43 Lahiri		
			♅℞ 02:59 UPh
	♆℞ 02:44 Vis		ASC 17:53 Has
			☋ 25:18 Cht
4th h. 31	3rd h. 32	2nd h. 24	1st h. 21

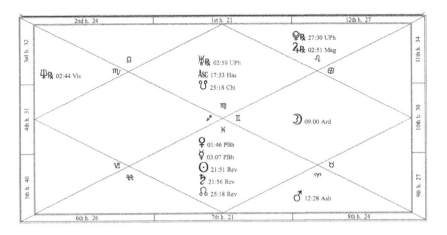

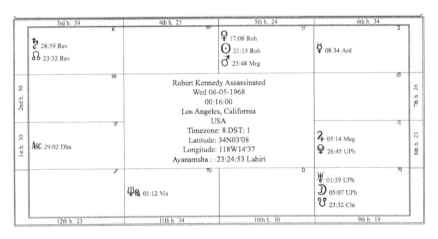

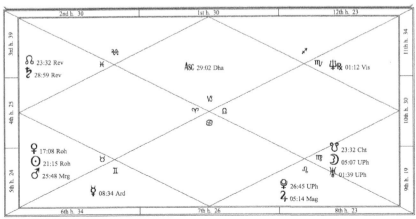

Chart 1 — Hurricane Katrina

6th h. 29	7th h. 31	8th h. 32	9th h. 25
☊ 20:25 Rev	♂ 22:18 Dha		☽ 17:06 Ard
♅℞ 14:56 Sat (5th h. 29)	Hurricane Katrina Mon 08-29-2005 12:00:00 New Orleans, Louisiana USA Timezone: 6 DST: 1 Latitude: 29N57'17 Longitude: 90W04'30 Ayanamsha : -23:56:07 Lahiri	♄ 11:37 Pus ☿ 25:46 Asl (10th h. 34)	
♆℞ 21:42 Shr (4th h. 27)		☉ 12:30 Mag (11th h. 28)	
3rd h. 27	♀℞ 27:53 Jye (2nd h. 29)	ASC 21:37 Vis (1st h. 24)	☋ 20:25 Has ♀ 20:55 Has ♃ 24:08 Cht (12th h. 22)

Chart — North Indian style (Katrina)

2nd h. 29	1st h. 24	12th h. 22
♀℞ 27:53 Jye ♏ (3rd h. 27)	ASC 21:37 Vis	♃ 24:08 Cht ♀ 20:55 Has ☋ 20:25 Has ♍ (11th h. 28)
♆℞ 21:42 Shr (4th h. 27)	♎ ♑ ⊕ ♈	☊ ☉ 12:30 Mag (10th h. 34) ☿ 25:46 Asl ♄ 11:37 Pus
♅℞ 14:56 Sat ♒ (5th h. 29) ♓ ☊ 20:25 Rev	♂ 22:18 Bha	♊ ☽ 17:06 Ard ♉ (9th h. 25)
6th h. 29	7th h. 31	8th h. 32

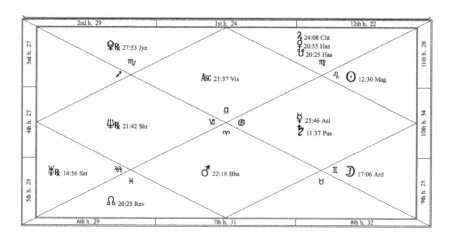

Chart 2 — Titanic

9th h. 21	10th h. 32	11th h. 25	12th h. 26
☊ 28:56 Rev ♀ 11:09 UBh ☽ 10:59 UBh	☿℞ 02:24 Ash ☉ 02:43 Ash ♄ 27:12 Kri		♀ 04:32 Mrg ♂ 12:57 Ard ♆ 28:24 Pun
(8th h. 32)	Titanic Mon 04-15-1912 12:00:00 New York, New York USA Timezone: 5 DST: 0 Latitude: 40N42'51 Longitude: 74W00'22 Ayanamsha : -22:37:48 Lahiri	ASC 15:48 Pus (1st h. 27)	
♅ 10:37 Shr (7th h. 33)			(2nd h. 31)
6th h. 29	♃℞ 22:27 Jye (5th h. 24)	4th h. 25	☋ 28:56 Cht (3rd h. 32)

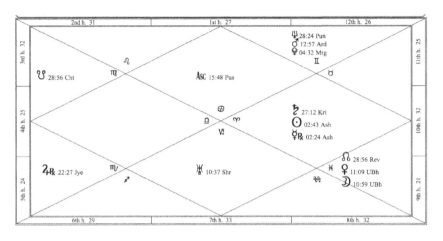

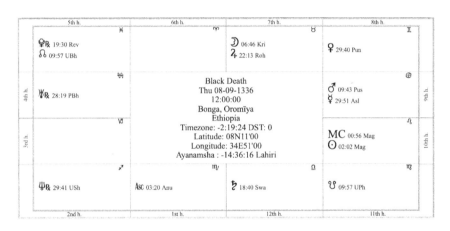

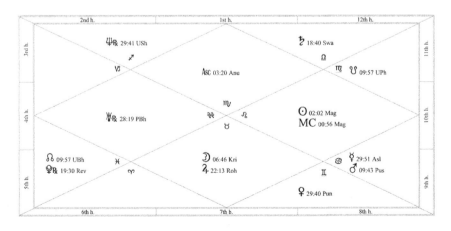

The Black Death was a devastating global epidemic of bubonic plague that struck Europe and Asia. The Black Death killed more than 20 million people in Europe, which was almost one-third of the continent's population.

On March 7, 1876, Alexander Graham Bell successfully received a patent for the telephone and secured the rights to the discovery. Days later, he made the first ever telephone call to his partner, Thomas Watson.

Rahu was in Pisces and Ketu in Virgo and Jupiter was aspecting (trine) Rahu. Rahu in Pisces and Ketu in Virgo has indicated invention and discoveries in healing. In this case it gave the ability for all people to connect through communications. This was the beginning of mass communications.

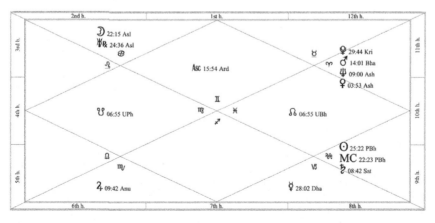

Catastrophic Events Rahu in Pisces and Ketu in Virgo

- Titanic sinking, Titanic sank after hitting an iceberg, April 15, 1912, killing 1517
- Korean War, war between North and South Korea, June 25, 1950, killing 2.5 million
- Hurricane Katrina, hurricane devastated New Orleans and Gulf Coast, August 29, 2005, killing 1800
- Kashmir earthquake in Pakistan, October 8, 2005, killing 87000
- Mumbai flood, flooding in Mumbai due to heavy rains, July 26, 2005, killing 1094

Predictions for November 28, 2023 – May 29, 2025: Rahu in Pisces and Ketu in Virgo

Two very important conjunctions this year are February 03, 2025, Rahu conjunct Neptune and April 20, 2025, Rahu conjunct Saturn.

Transiting Saturn and Neptune are conjunct Rahu in Pisces in the nakshatra Purva Bhadrapada which indicates "the man with two faces." There is deep deception concerning a person who pretends to be someone or something else other than how they appear to the world. Also, Neptune is around 6° Pisces conjunct the fixed star Scheat, one of the worst stars and represents tragic events.

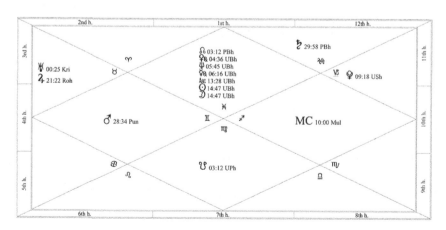

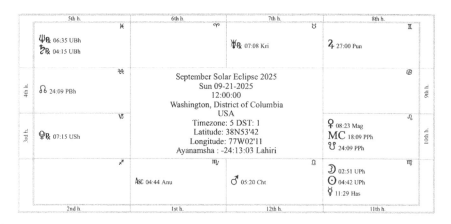

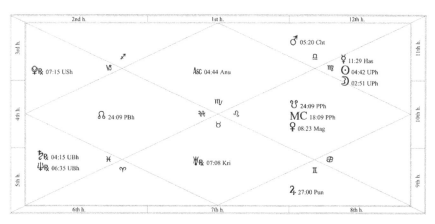

Outer planets conjunct the nodes are the number one indicator of big events. These three planets indicate world events as they are transpersonal. In other words, they indicate events that affect the masses and produce events that are long range. Next, the aspects of either Saturn or Jupiter will affect the results of the events especially concerning the economy. But when there is a conjunction of the nodes with an outer planet and especially Saturn or Jupiter there is always a huge event. This year 2025 has both Saturn and an outer planet (Neptune) conjunct the nodes and eclipses.

As mentioned before, the last time Saturn and Rahu was conjunct in the sign Pisces was 1968 which was a horrendous year as both

Martin Luther King Jr and Robert Kennedy were assassinated. Furthermore, it was the worst time for the Vietnam war as many American soldiers died in this year. Saturn was conjunct Rahu when President Lincoln was assassinated but they were in Libra. This period is none the less a very dangerous time politically in the world. Saturn and Rahu are together in Pisces from March 29 – May 29, 2025.

During the 2016 elections with Donald Trump and Hillary Clinton competing, Ketu was conjunct Neptune (but in Aquarius) during this time, indicating the deception and surprise over the elections with Donald Trump the winner. Neptune tends to be blinding and indicates confusion, and the inability to see clearly.

On the day of the solar eclipse March 29, 2025, Saturn will transit into the sign of Pisces. From March 29 – May 29, 2025, Rahu and Saturn will be conjunct. Remember the nodes are everything about what is going on in the world. This eclipse involves Saturn, Rahu, Neptune, retrograde Venus, and retrograde Mercury, with the Sun and Moon. This is groundbreaking! This is one of the most eventful times in history.

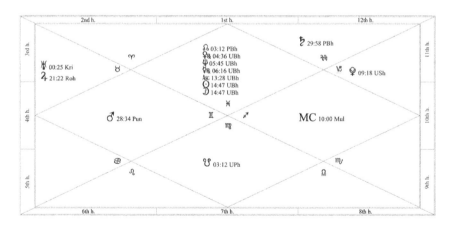

Transiting Saturn is trine Mars, which is a strong aspect according to Nadi astrology. This connects Mars and Saturn in air signs which pertains to communications and travel by air. Mars as it transits through Gemini indicates difficult weather.

Many planets are in Pisces in the Nakshatra Uttara Bhadrapada except Rahu is in Purva Bhadrapada. This sign points to the oceans and seas, which will indicate many events concerning the waters. The Bhadrapadas are the two nakshatras of the funeral cot. Purva Bhadrapada is the front end of the funeral cot while Uttara Bhadrapada is the back end of the funeral cot. This can indicate situations around death and funerals. This may be indicative of a time when there is destruction and death on the planet. In 1968 when Saturn and Rahu were in Pisces there was massive death in Vietnam as well as the assassination of two great leaders Martin Luther King Jr and Robert Kennedy.

Venus and Jupiter are in Parivartana (mutual exchange of signs). Venus is in Pisces ruled by Jupiter and Jupiter is in Taurus ruled by Venus. This connects these two planets. These two benefic planets can indicate wealth and prosperity during this time, as Venus is in its most powerful sign of exaltation.

Venus, Mercury, and Neptune are all within a degree conjunct the most difficult fixed star Scheat. This star indicates tragedy. For those with a Leo ascendant or natal Moon this Stellium of planets is transiting the 8th house which is the most difficult house in a chart and can indicate endings and death. Two politicians with Leo Ascendant are President Trump and Vice President J.D. Vance, and Elon Musk has a Moon in Leo. Can this be foretelling a tragedy in the USA? In the USA birth chart this Stellium is in the 4th house indicating problems with the homeland, could there be an attack on the USA?

Transiting Mars is retrograde from December 6, 2024 to February 24, 2025. From January 20, 2025 to April 3, 2025, Mars will be in Gemini. This truly exacerbates the difficult events for the USA because Mars will be transiting the most important planets in the USA natal chart. The fact that Mars will station on the USA Sun (22°) February 24, 2025, can represent violence for the President. This time is critical in terms of the events occurring in the USA.

Chart 1 (North Indian / South Indian style square chart)

1st h.	2nd h.	3rd h.	4th h.
♀ 16:02 UBh Asc 09:02 UBh ♆ 04:31 UBh ☊ 03:21 UBh ♓	♈ ♅ 29:19 Kri	♉ ♃ 17:44 Roh	♊ ♂ 22:48 Pun
12th h. ♄ 25:56 PBh ☿ 24:19 PBh ☉ 11:57 Sat ♒	Mars Stations Mon 02-24-2025 07:57:17 Washington, District of Columbia USA Timezone: 5 DST: 0 Latitude: 38N53'42 Longitude: 77W02'11 Ayanamsha : -24:12:32 Lahiri		5th h. ♋
11th h. ♀ 08:33 USh ♑			6th h. ♌
♐ ☽ 26:22 PSh MC 07:34 Mul	♏	♎ ☋ 03:21 UPh	♍ ♎
10th h.	9th h.	8th h.	7th h.

Chart 2 (South Indian diamond chart)

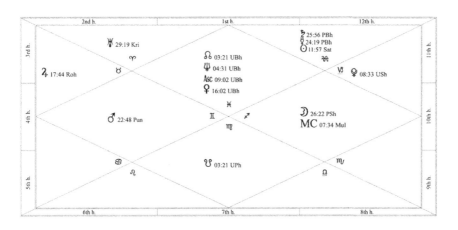

2nd h.	1st h.	12th h.
♅ 29:19 Kri	☊ 03:21 UBh ♆ 04:31 UBh ASC 09:02 UBh ♀ 16:02 UBh	♄ 25:56 PBh ☿ 24:19 PBh ☉ 11:57 Sat

3rd h. — ♈
♃ 17:44 Roh — ♉ — ♓ ♑ — ♀ 08:33 USh — 11th h.

4th h. — ♂ 22:48 Pun — ♊ — ♐ — ☽ 26:22 PSh / MC 07:34 Mul — 10th h.

5th h. — ♋ ♌ — ♍ — ☋ 03:21 UPh — ♏ — ♎ — 9th h.

6th h. — 7th h. — 8th h.

Chart 3

USA
Thu 07-04-1776
18:30:00
Philadelphia, PA,Pennsylvania
USA
Timezone: 5 DST: 0
Latitude: 39N57'08
Longitude: 75W09'51
Ayanamsha : -20:43:59 Lahiri

4th h.	5th h.	6th h.	7th h.
♓	♈ ♅ 18:11 Roh	♉	♊ ♂ 00:40 Mrg ☿ 12:26 Ard ♃ 15:12 Ard ☉ 22:38 Pun
3rd h. ☽ 07:14 Sat ♒			8th h. ♋ ♀℞ 03:26 Pus ☊ 15:51 Pus
2nd h. ☋ 15:51 Shr ♀℞ 06:49 USh ♑			9th h. ♌
♐ ASC 08:50 Mul	♏ MC 01:49 Cht	♎ ♆ 01:41 UPh ♄ 24:04 Cht	♍
1st h.	12th h.	11th h.	10th h.

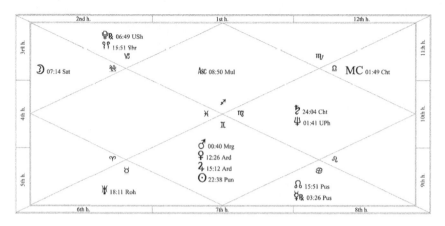

May 29, 2025, Rahu will transit into Aquarius and Ketu into Leo. They will remain in these signs for about 18 months until September 8, 2027. During this time Jupiter will be in Gemini from May 14, 2025 to October 18, 2025. It will whiz through the entire sign of Gemini but then station retrograde at 0° Cancer November 11, 2025, and return to Gemini December 12 ,2025 and remain there until June 1, 2026. So, transiting Jupiter is 0° Cancer from October 18, 2025 to December 12, 2025. This will bring enormous healing as this is Jupiter's best sign of exaltation and can represent good things occurring around the world. This is much needed after all the chaos of 2024 and 2025. Jupiter will then enter and stay in Cancer from June 1, 2026 to June 26, 2027. This will be a golden era!

CHAPTER 3

Rahu in Aquarius and Ketu in Leo

May 29, 2025 to November 25, 2026

Looking back, this was a time of great discovery and inventions. It was also a time of great destruction and terrorism, along with tremendous revolts that killed many.

Nakshatras Activated

Rahu in Aquarius (Dhanishta, Shatabhishak, Purva Bhadrapada) and Ketu in Leo (Magha, Purva Phalguni, Uttara Phalguni).

What happened before:

The Tiananmen Square Massacre of 1989 occurred with Rahu in Aquarius and Ketu in Leo. The student-led demonstrations in Beijing were forcibly suppressed after the government declared martial law, and troops with assault rifles and tanks killed thousands of demonstrators trying to block the military's advance into Tiananmen Square.

Joni Patry

Rahu and Ketu in the signs of Aquarius and Leo frequently point to governments in opposition to their own people or humanity.

The PanAm airline crash over Lockerbie Scotland, on December 21, 1988, was an early terrorist attack. Rahu was in Aquarius in the nakshatra Shatabhishak, which is ruled by Rahu. It appears that when Rahu transits nakshatras ruled by Rahu, the results can be treacherous especially for air travel. Rahu-ruled nakshatras (Ardra, Swati and Shatabhishak) are in air signs Gemini, Libra, and Aquarius.

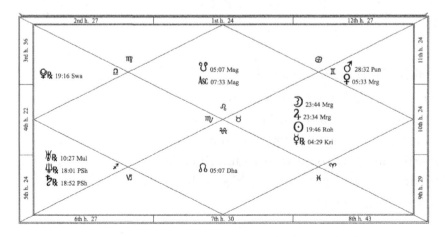

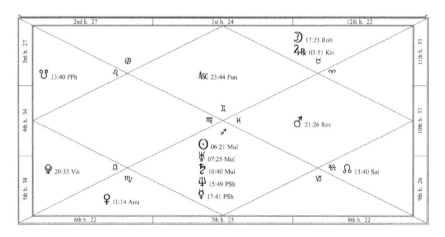

	10th h. 37	11th h. 33	12th h. 22	1st h. 24	
	♂ 21:26 Rev		♃Rx 03:51 Kri ☽ 17:23 Roh	ASC 23:44 Pun	
9th h. 26	☊ 13:40 Sat	1988 Pan Am Airline crash Wed 12-21-1988 17:03:00 Lockerbie, Borders Scotland Timezone: 0 DST: 0 Latitude: 55N07'00 Longitude: 03W22'00 Ayanamsha : -23:42:17 Lahiri			2nd h. 27
8th h. 22				☋ 13:40 PPh	3rd h. 27
	☿ 17:41 PSh ♆ 15:49 PSh ♄ 10:40 Mul ♅ 07:25 Mul ☉ 06:21 Mul	♀ 11:14 Anu	♀ 20:33 Vis		
	7th h. 25	6th h. 22	5th h. 38	4th h. 34	

South Indian chart:

	2nd h. 27	1st h. 24	12th h. 22	
3rd h. 27	☋ 13:40 PPh ⊕	ASC 23:44 Pun	☽ 17:23 Roh ♃Rx 03:51 Kri	11th h. 33
4th h. 34		♂ 21:26 Rev	10th h. 37
5th h. 38	♀ 20:33 Vis	☉ 06:21 Mul ♅ 07:25 Mul ♄ 10:40 Mul ♆ 15:49 PSh ☿ 17:41 PSh	☊ 13:40 Sat	9th h. 26
	♀ 11:14 Anu	7th h. 25	8th h. 22	
	6th h. 22			

The last time Rahu was in Leo and Ketu in Aquarius there were amazing inventions such as in 2007 the Apple iPhone came out. This revolutionized the world and allowed everyone to connect to each other through a technology that they could hold in their hand. During this time Rahu was conjunct Uranus, the planet of inventions.

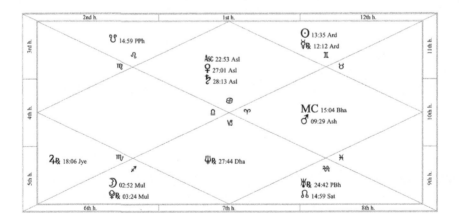

Also, on July 23, 1969, the USA put a man on the Moon for the first time and on that day, Pluto was conjunct Ketu and Uranus was conjunct Jupiter both exactly. Also transiting Mars was conjunct Neptune indicating developments beyond this world.

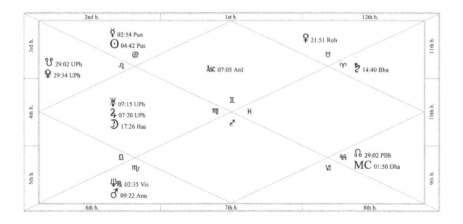

American astronaut Neil Armstrong became the first person to walk on the Moon. He stepped out of the Apollo 11 lunar module and onto the Moon's surface, in an area called the 'Sea of Tranquility.

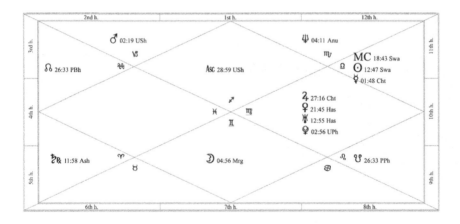

North Indian chart (top):

4th h.	5th h.	6th h.	7th h.
♓ ♄℞ 11:58 Ash	♈	♉ ☽ 04:56 Mrg	♊

3rd h. ♒ ☊ 26:33 PBh	Internet Invented Wed 10-29-1969 12:00:00 Los Angeles, California USA Timezone: 8 DST: 0 Latitude: 34N03'08 Longitude: 118W14'37 Ayanamsha : -23:26:10 Lahiri		8th h. ♋
2nd h. ♑ ♂ 02:19 USh		♌ ☋ 26:33 PPh	9th h.
1st h. ♐ ASC 28:59 USh	♏ ♆ 04:11 Anu	♎ ☿ 01:48 Cht ☉ 12:47 Swa MC 18:43 Swa	♍ ♀ 02:56 UPh ♅ 12:55 Has ♀ 21:45 Has ♃ 27:16 Cht
1st h.	12th h.	11th h.	10th h.

South Indian chart (bottom):

2nd h. ♂ 02:19 USh ♑	1st h.	12th h. ♆ 04:11 Anu ♏
3rd h. ☊ 26:33 PBh ♒	ASC 28:59 USh	MC 18:43 Swa ♎ ☉ 12:47 Swa ☿ 01:48 Cht
4th h.	♓ ♐ ♏ ♊	10th h. ♃ 27:16 Cht ♀ 21:45 Has ♅ 12:55 Has ♀ 02:56 UPh
5th h. ♄℞ 11:58 Ash ♈ ♉	7th h. ☽ 04:56 Mrg	8th h. ♌ ☋ 26:33 PPh ♋
6th h.	7th h.	8th h.

On October 29, 1969, the internet was invented at UCLA, where the first message was sent over the ARPANET. This first message was sent from UCLA's Interface Message Processor (IMP) at Stanford Research Institute. The message was sent by a team of students led by Leonard Kleinrock, a computer science professor at UCLA.

So much happened in 1969 including putting a man on the Moon, as well as the true beginning of the internet. During this year Jupiter was in the same sign (Virgo) with Pluto and Uranus, indicating massive inventions that changed the world forever. Rahu was in Leo and Ketu in Aquarius, which these two signs are notorious for great events that changed the world.

Catastrophic events with Rahu in Aquarius and Ketu in Leo

- World War I began with Ketu in Leo and Rahu in Aquarius on July 18, 1914, killing 15 -20 million people. Saturn and Pluto were tightly conjunct in Gemini.
- Bhola Cyclone – This cyclone killed hundreds of Thousands in East Pakistan on November 13, 1970. Approximately 300,000 – 500,000 people were killed.
- Armenian Earthquake December 7, 1988 killed 25,000 and Saturn, Uranus, and Neptune were conjunct in Sagittarius.
- The Tiananmen Square Massacre in1989 Killed several thousand
- The PanAm airline crash over Lockerbie Scotland on December 21, 1988, killed 270 people.

Predictions for Rahu in Aquarius and Ketu in Leo – May 29, 2025 to November 25, 2026

On February 17, 2026, there is a solar eclipse in Aquarius with Rahu. Jupiter is in Gemini aspecting (trine) Rahu throughout the year. Jupiter's aspect to Rahu is where they mutually aspect each other and represent expansion, prosperity, and luck. As both are in air signs there will be major expansion with developments in communications and travel.

Venus and Rahu or exactly conjunct at 14° of Aquarius in the nakshatra Shatabishak, which pertains to the 100 healers. I believe with Rahu in this nakshatra, incredible discoveries will be made with regards to healing modalities and medicines. This is the future of a new frontier in medicine, health, and new forms of healing. Great strides and discoveries will be made in mental disease particularly around the area of addictions.

Saturn and Neptune will transit together around 6° to 7° of Pisces June to August 2025 then exactly conjunct at 6° of Pisces February 20, 2026. This degree is conjunct the fixed star Scheat, which can pertain to tragedies. In Pisces this may pertain to problems with the oceans, pointing towards drowning and possibly with tsunamis or floods. Saturn represents reality while Neptune represents illusions, and this can be indicative of uncovering illusions or deceptions. Jupiter rules Pisces therefore it is the dispositor of both Saturn and Neptune while they are in Pisces. This connects Jupiter to Saturn and Neptune, and while Jupiter is in Gemini, this means there will be problems with communications and travel. Airlines and mass computer outages will be an issue.

Therefore, truths will be uncovered concerning the communications which points to the corruption of the media, highlighting the truth about where the propaganda is coming from.

Overall, this is a time for great inventions and discoveries with the invention of the iPhone and putting a man on the Moon for the first time. These discoveries will again pertain to travelling into space as well as technology with air travel. There will be great strides and accomplishments in the area of health and healing for very difficult diseases, and this will also promote longevity for mankind.

The most significant trends will involve a better understanding of mental disease. I believe Rahu's most powerful placement is in Aquarius. I also believe this is Rahu's exaltation sign because Rahu prospers in air signs and Aquarius is ruled by Saturn. Rahu and Saturn in Vedic astrology are said to be likened to one another.

Both Saturn and Neptune rule oil. Saturn rules crude oil and Neptune rules oil and natural gas. As they come together especially at this degree of tragedy and sorrow 6° of Pisces (fixed star Scheat), we can expect tragedies concerning oil spills and explosions. Oil will be used as a manipulative tool to cripple many countries. This could also affect the price of oil and gas, with problems like these the prices could escalate.

Rahu in Aquarius is a time of great invention and while Jupiter is in Gemini, pertaining to travel there will be discoveries in the way we travel. The use of propulsion instead of fire to ignite engines or rockets (combustion) will begin a new age of travel.

2nd h.		3rd h.		4th h.		5th h.	
	♓		♈		♉		♊
♆ 06:25 UBh ♄ 06:09 UBh				⛢ 03:18 Kri		♃℞ 21:37 Pun	
	♒	February Solar Eclipse 26					♋
℞ 22:26 PBh ℞ 14:43 Sat ℞ 14:37 Sat ℞ 04:36 Dha ℞ 04:29 Dha ℞ 04:25 Dha		Tue 02-17-2026 07:00:42 Washington, District of Columbia USA					
	♑	Timezone: 5 DST: 0 Latitude: 38N53'42					♌
♂ 25:27 Dha ♀ 09:58 USh		Longitude: 77W02'11 Ayanamsha : -24:13:27 Lahiri				☋ 14:43 PPh	
	♐		♍		♎		♏
		MC 17:53 Jye					
11th h.		10th h.		9th h.		8th h.	

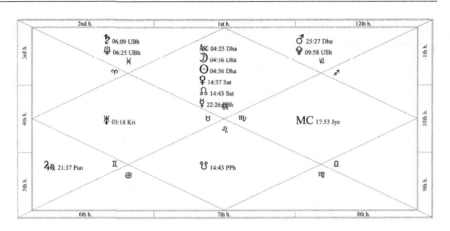

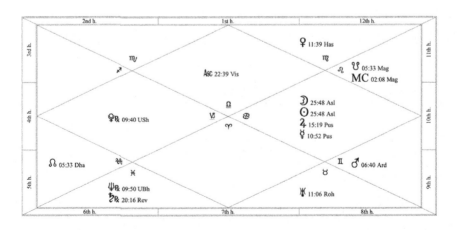

CHAPTER 4

Rahu in Capricorn and Ketu in Cancer

November 25, 2026 to May 24, 2028

When Rahu is in Capricorn and Ketu in Cancer there were indications of peace and healing as this was when the Berlin Wall came down. There were also other indications of peace and healing during these times. There were financial difficulties probably due to the placement of Ketu in Cancer as it would be in the 8th house of government money for the USA chart. Also, there was an advancement in technology with the Hubble Space Telescope that was launched into space. I have high hopes for the year of 2027 to reenact some of the healing potential of Rahu and Ketu in these signs.

Nakshatras Activated

Rahu in Capricorn (Uttara Aashaadha, Shraavana, Dhanishta) and Ketu in Cancer (Punarvasu, Pushya, Ashlesha).

What happened before:

The Berlin Wall came down on November 9, 1989, when Rahu was at 28° Capricorn, and Ketu was in Cancer. This was a day of healing and reunification for homeland Germany, and a new era for Europe if not the world.

The stock market crash in 2008 had a devastating effect on the U.S economy. This event threatened the financial security of the USA because the country's birth chart for the USA has these very placements in the 8th house of scandals. Rahu was in Capricorn conjunct Neptune, but no one saw this one coming. Neptune with Rahu indicates deception and corruption. Many got away with millions in profits, with no consequences. Enormous scandals were rampant during this time.

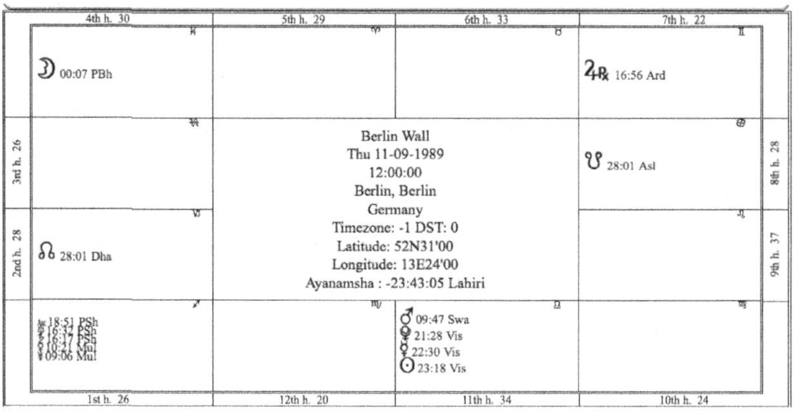

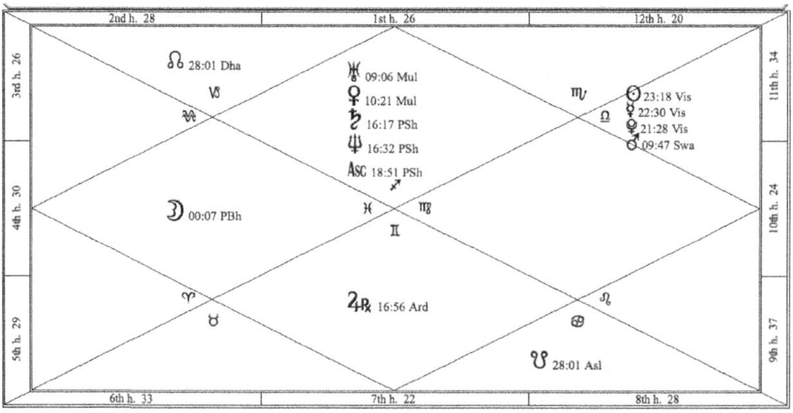

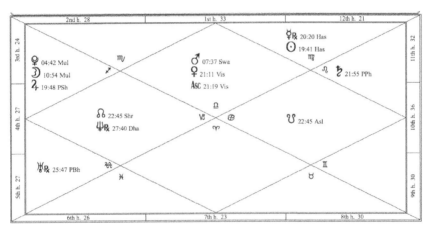

Even though there was a stock market crash in the year of 2008 while Rahu was in Capricorn and Ketu was in Cancer, I believe that the year of 2027 will be more prosperous because Ketu will be transiting with Jupiter in the sign of Cancer, which is Jupiter's most powerful placement as it is exalted here.

Major events and crises

- 2008 Financial crisis.
- Technology: Intel released the 4004, the world's first microprocessor. The first arcade video game, Computer Space, was released in November or December. Ray Tomlinson sent the first ARPAnet email, using the @ sign in an address.
- The fall of the Soviet Union: The Baltic states declared independence from the Soviet Union during Perestroika.
- The reunification of Germany: Germany was reunited after 45 years of separation.
- The launch of the Hubble Space Telescope: The Hubble Space Telescope was launched into space on April 24, 1990.
- Bangladesh Liberation War – war for Liberation from Pakistan -March 26, 1971, killed approximately 3 million people.
- California Earthquake near San Francisco (Loma Prieta) October 17, 1989, killed 63 people.
- Iran Earthquake June 21, 1980, Killed 50,000 people.
- Kuwait – Iraq war August 2, 1990.
- Sichuan Earthquake in China May 12, 2008, killed 87,000 people.
- Cyclone Nargis in Myanmar May 2, 2008, killed 138,000 people.
- Hurricane Ike affected the Texas coast September 1, 2008, killed 138,000 people.

Predictions for November 25, 2026 to May 24, 2028 - Rahu in Capricorn and Ketu in Cancer

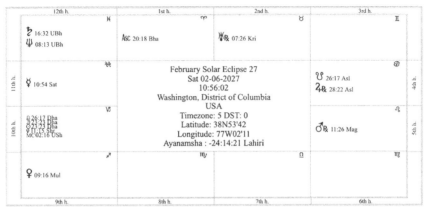

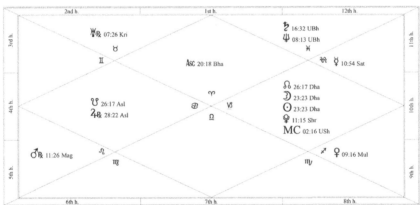

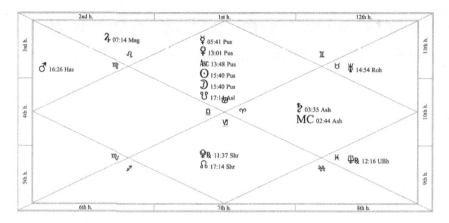

Whenever Ketu is conjunct a benefic and that benefic is in a powerful sign, it indicates very positive events that will manifest. Jupiter is the most benefic planet, and it is in it's most powerful sign of exaltation, which is Cancer, indicating this is a sign of great things to come this year.

Since both Jupiter and Ketu indicate spirituality, this could mean that in 2027 many people will be searching for meaning and truth in their lives. This could represent a quest or movement towards things more spiritual, heightening the consciousness of the planet. All things surrounding higher consciousness and spiritual development will be in the news. Motivational speakers, psychological studies, and spiritual awareness groups become a theme and a focus within the media.

There will be amazing revelations that surface and many truths about corruption that have taken place around the world, but especially in the USA. As the truth is revealed a major healing will take place. This is due to Jupiter with Ketu transiting the sign of Cancer in the 8th House of the USA chart. The 8th house deals with big money, corruption, secrets, and transformation. Pluto is also with Rahu; therefore, the effects will be gigantic and will restore the foundation of what the USA was originally founded upon.

The nakshatra that Rahu is in is Dhanishta which indicates the "richest one," this insinuates that this is a time of wealth and prosperity. But as Jupiter and Ketu are in the nakshatra Ashlesha, this can deal with new ways of healing along the lines of raising consciousness. Ashlesha has been likened to kundalini energy, which is considered to be the ultimate life force and the source of our creative power and spiritual gifts. There will be new tools for higher consciousness pertaining to hypnosis and mind control techniques that raise consciousness and awareness.

March and April of 2027 will be dangerous for severe weather concerning floods and storms. During this time Mars will be retrograde in Cancer close to Jupiter and Ketu. As Mars retrogrades back over the gandanta degree of 29° of Cancer around April 25th, 2027, look out for very dangerous storms.

The Berlin wall coming down and the reunification of Germany was in 1989 and in 1990 Jupiter was conjunct Ketu in Cancer indicating this was a powerful time for healing around the world. In 2027 it will again be a time for unity and healing as Jupiter and Ketu will converge in the same sign of Cancer.

June 2, 2027, Saturn will enter the sign of Aries which is its debilitation sign. It will remain in Aries until it retrogrades back into Pisces October 19, 2027. While Saturn is in Aries for four months there will be problems for governments and disorganization along with social uprisings. This leads to upheaval, strife, and rebellion around the world.

July 31, 2026, Jupiter will enter Leo and conjunct Ketu, but Jupiter will retrograde back into Cancer January 24, 2027 – June 26, 2027, therefore Jupiter will be with Ketu in Cancer during this time. This can be an awakening on a spiritual level. It will also be a major transformation of a great magnitude as Rahu is in Capricorn.

CHAPTER 5

Rahu in Sagittarius and Ketu in Gemini

May 24, 2028 to February 4, 2030

This is the flip side of a treacherous placement for Rahu and Ketu, because here we have Ketu in Gemini in the tragic nakshatra of Ardra. Rahu will be in the destructive nakshatra of Mula. One of the most destructive earthquakes in history was in Japan on March 11, 2011. Rahu was in Mula at 4° Sagittarius conjunct the Galactic Center. What seems to come out of such tragedy is the clearing away for the new, but it still causes much human suffering.

Nakshatras Activated

Rahu in Sagittarius (Mula, Purva Ashadha, Uttara Ashadha) and Ketu in Gemini (Mrigashira, Ardra, Punarvasu).

What happened before:

Extreme pandemics, earthquakes, and tsunamis, along with severe weather dominated the world events. This is one of the most dangerous axis for Rahu and Ketu to be in. The reversal of this where Rahu is in Gemini and Ketu in Sagittarius has proven to be the most dangerous with the most catastrophic events. I have noted that the reversal of this activates similar events.

The 9.1-magnitude earthquake northeast of Tokyo, the largest to hit Japan, caused a tsunami with 30-foot waves that damaged several nuclear reactors in the area. The combined total of confirmed deaths and missing was more than 22,000 people.

In the 1918 pandemic that killed over 50 million people, Rahu was in Sagittarius and Ketu in Gemini. Here again, this treacherous portion of the zodiac is tragically vulnerable to transits of Rahu and Ketu that cause disasters for many.

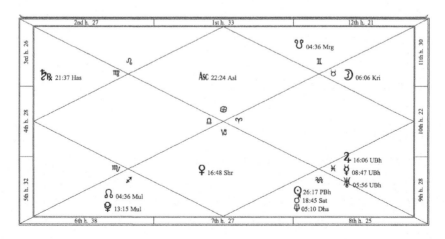

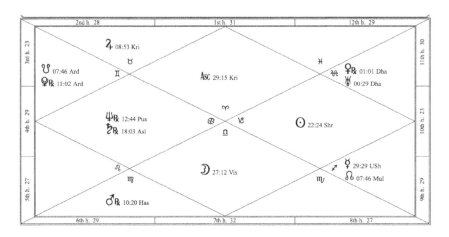

12th h. 29	1st h. 31	2nd h. 28	3rd h. 23
	ASC 29:15 Kri	♃ 08:53 Kri	☋ 07:46 Ard / ♀℞ 11:02 Ard
11th h. 30 — ♀℞ 01:01 Dha / ⚸ 00:29 Dha	Pandemic Mon 02-04-1918 12:00:00 Dallas, Texas USA Timezone: 6 DST: 0 Latitude: 32N46'59 Longitude: 96W48'24 Ayanamsha : -22:43:06 Lahiri		♅℞ 12:44 Pus / ♄℞ 18:03 Asl — 4th h. 29
10th h. 23 — ☉ 22:24 Shr			5th h. 27
☿ 29:29 USh / ☊ 07:46 Mul		☽ 27:12 Vis	♂℞ 10:20 Has
9th h. 29	8th h. 27	7th h. 32	6th h. 29

It appears that there was an enormous number of earthquakes and volcanic eruptions during this time. Another tragedy that affected this time pertained to the 1918 flu pandemic killing between 50 to 100 million people.

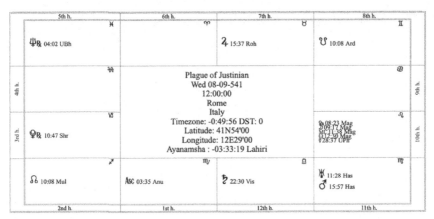

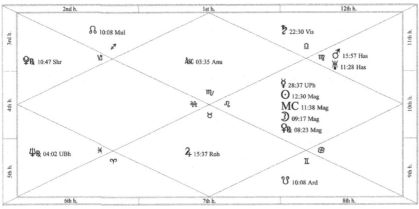

This plague spread east to the Caucasus, infecting and invading Persian armies throughout Europe where it became endemic. With localized outbreaks occurring for the next two centuries, disappearing entirely by the year 750. However, the worst was over by the year 590. It is impossible to be certain of the mortality rate during this outbreak. Estimates vary between 25 million and 100 million deaths, but approximately one third of Europe's population had been wiped out. Not until that latter plague ravaged Europe would a pandemic on the scale of the plague of Justinian be experienced again.

Therefore, based on this information we can speculate Rahu in Sagittarius and Ketu in Gemini points to events with earthquakes, volcanic eruptions, and pandemics.

Best time for the economy in the USA was the 1950s, as it was the boom time after World War II. It was documented that 1954 was the best of all year for the golden years. During this time Rahu was in Sagittarius and Ketu in Gemini. The most significant aspect during this time was Ketu with Jupiter and Uranus causing a great expansive boom. The nodal axis in Gemini and Sagittarius is the most eventual of all the signs.

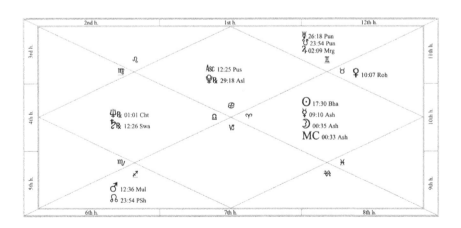

Major Crises and Events

- Earthquake in Haiti January 12th, 2010, killed 220,000 – 316,000 people.
- Earthquake and Tsunami in Japan March 11, 2011, killed 15,897 people.
- Earthquake in Chile February 27, 2010, killed 525 people.
- Severe volcanic eruption in Iceland April 14, 2010, disrupted air travel.
- Bosnian war, ethnic conflict in Bosnia and Herzegovina April 6, 1992, killed 100,000 people.
- Hurricane Andrew, hurricane in Florida and Louisiana August 24, 1992, killed 65 people.
- Bangladesh cyclone April 29, 1991, killed 138,000 people.
- Volcanic eruption in the Philippines June 15, 1991, killed 800 people.
- Syrian civil war March 15, 2011, killed 500,000 people.

Predictions for May 24, 2028 to February 4, 2030 - Rahu in Sagittarius and Ketu in Gemini

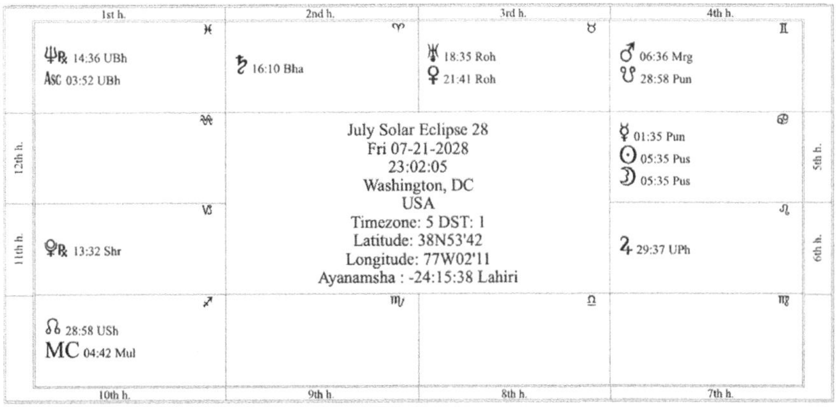

1st h.	2nd h.	3rd h.	4th h.
♄ 27:47 Rev ASC 16:14 UBh Ψ 10:06 UBh ♓	♈	♅℞ 11:48 Roh ♉	♊
♀ 21:47 PBh ♒	January Solar eclipse 28 Wed 01-26-2028 10:11:29 Washington, District of Columbia USA	☋ 08:07 Pus	♋
☿ 24:59 Dha ☉ 23:50 Dha ♀ 11:55 Shr ☽ 11:55 Shr ☊ 08:07 USh ♑	Timezone: 5 DST: 0 Latitude: 38N53'42 Longitude: 77W02'11 Ayanamsha : -24:15:13 Lahiri		♌
MC 11:31 Mul ♐	♏	♎	2₄℞ 02:55 UPh ♍
10th h.	9th h.	8th h.	7th h.

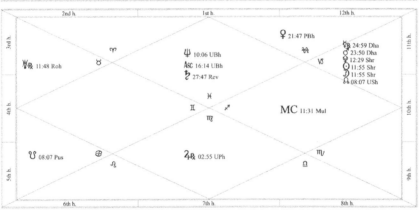

1st h.	2nd h.	3rd h.	4th h.
Ψ℞ 14:36 UBh ASC 03:52 UBh ♓	♄ 16:10 Bha ♈	♅ 18:35 Roh ♀ 21:41 Roh ♉	♂ 06:36 Mrg ☋ 28:58 Pun ♊
♒	July Solar Eclipse 28 Fri 07-21-2028 23:02:05 Washington, DC USA	☿ 01:35 Pun ☉ 05:35 Pus ☽ 05:35 Pus ♋	
♀℞ 13:32 Shr ♑	Timezone: 5 DST: 1 Latitude: 38N53'42 Longitude: 77W02'11 Ayanamsha : -24:15:38 Lahiri	2₄ 29:37 UPh	♌
☊ 28:58 USh MC 04:42 Mul ♐	♍	♎	♍
10th h.	9th h.	8th h.	7th h.

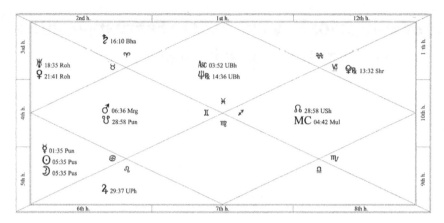

There may be indications of a flu or pandemic again. When Jupiter is in Virgo, and Mars is in Gemini conjunct Ketu July – August 2028. As Jupiter moves swiftly into the sign of Virgo it will transit through the entire sign from July 24, 2028 to December 26, 2028. It speeds through the entire sign of Virgo in five months. But it will retrograde back where it will stay in Virgo from March 29, 2029 to August 24, 2029. It is unusual how fast Jupiter is moving. This may indicate that many affairs ruled by Jupiter are evolving. This indicates there is expansion in health and healing modalities probably because there are health issues that arise. However, there will be cures that are discovered as an outcome.

Major shifts and changes are occurring in the government of the USA as Ketu is transiting over all the planets that are in Gemini in the chart for the USA (Mars, Jupiter, Venus, and Sun). Jupiter will be transiting over Saturn in the 10th House of the USA chart indicating that there will be positive changes in the government and leadership. There seems to be a new guard that will lead and change the government in the USA. This is the year that a new President is elected, and the outcome appears to be very good for the USA.

Saturn is debilitated in Aries and is fully aspecting Ketu with its third full aspect. This adds to the great difficulty of the problems Ketu in

Gemini will manifest. This is probably due to the issues around health and pointing to catastrophes concerning the economy.

As Mars comes together with Ketu around August 24, 2028, there will be volcanic eruptions as well as earthquakes occurring around the world. This could most definitely affect the Western Coast of the USA, primarily California, during this time.

We are on the brink of radical shifts and changes that will eventually move us in the right direction, but great difficulties will develop before. This means we must go through purging that will initiate a healing. Moving towards the beginning of the year 2029 when Ketu is in the nakshatra Ardra and Rahu is in the nakshatra Mula, many problems that have been brewing will come to the surface and explode. This of course has many repercussions leading to problems like earthquakes and volcanic eruptions as well as disease and pandemics.

Predictions 2029

Throughout the year 2029 Jupiter will be moving extremely fast, but will stay primarily in the sign of Virgo. During this time Jupiter will be opposing Neptune and again this could indicate issues around pandemics and health.

Transiting Mars enters Virgo on December 8, 2028, and will remain there until July 27, 2029. It will be retrograde on February 14, 2029 to May 5, 2029. While Mars is retrograde in Virgo, it will bring out severe health issues in the form of a pandemic that will dominate this year. In 2014 Mars was retrograde in Virgo and this brought the Ebola virus into the USA.

This time while Mars is in Virgo it will be in opposition to Neptune. Mars will oppose Neptune three times while it moves back and forth in retrograde motion, January 3, 2029 Mars will oppose Neptune at

11° of Virgo/Pisces, March 16, 2029 Mars will oppose Neptune at 13° Virgo/Pisces and July 7, 2029 Mars will oppose Neptune at 16° Virgo/Pisces. Neptune indicates extremes with deception, deceit, scandals, illusions, and most of all disease.

While Mars is in Virgo it will be accompanied by Jupiter, which will magnify and make events bigger concerning the effects of a serious global disease. Transiting Jupiter will be in Virgo November 26, 2027 to February 28, 2028, then again July 24, 2028 to December 26, 2028, and again March 29, 2029 to August 24, 2029. Each time Jupiter is in Virgo it manifests and magnifies the potential of disease around the world. It will be opposing Neptune throughout this back-and-forth transit in Virgo. Jupiter opposing Neptune will manifest more deception, illusion, and surface mini scandals around what is behind the pandemic.

Around the June solar eclipse in 2029 Mars will be at the midpoint of Rahu and Ketu. This intensifies the power of Mars and intensifies the possibility for earthquakes and tsunamis as Neptune is at the other extreme opposing Mars, and Neptune has been known to indicate earthquakes.

April to August 2029, Rahu will be in the nakshatra Mula and Ketu will be in Ardra. These are the most difficult nakshatras for Rahu and Ketu to be in. Expect some devastating events that could cripple the world.

August 8, 2029, Saturn will transit into Taurus and August 24, 2029 Jupiter will transit into Libra. Jupiter and Saturn are in a quincunx aspect meaning they are 8 and 6 spacial relationships from one another. This is a very difficult aspect for Jupiter and Saturn since both planets are indicative of the economic situation in the world there is going to be a financial crisis. This is probably due to the health crisis as well as the major earth changes occurring around the world.

The June eclipse of the Sun and Moon in Taurus are conjunct Uranus, which is another indication of unexpected events. Uranus like Neptune rules earthquakes.

Chart 1 (North Indian / South Indian style)

12th h.	1st h.	2nd h.	3rd h.
♆ 12:03 UBh (ℋ)	♄ 10:13 Ash / ASC 20:16 Bha (♈)	♅℞ 16:23 Roh (♉)	☊ 19:45 Ard (♊)

11th h.			4th h.
(♒)	January Solar Eclipse 29		(♋)
	Sun 01-14-2029		
(♑)	12:24:24		(♌)
10th h.	Washington, District of Columbia		5th h.
♀ 13:43 Shr / ☿℞ 04:17 USh / MC 02:14 USh / ☽ 00:34 USh / ☉ 00:34 USh	USA		
	Timezone: 5 DST: 0		
	Latitude: 38N53'42		
	Longitude: 77W02'11		
	Ayanamsha : -24:16:04 Lahiri		

9th h.	8th h.	7th h.	6th h.
☋ 19:45 PSh / ♀ 14:01 PSh (♐)	(♍) ♃ 02:02 Cht	(♎)	(♏) ♂ 14:41 Has

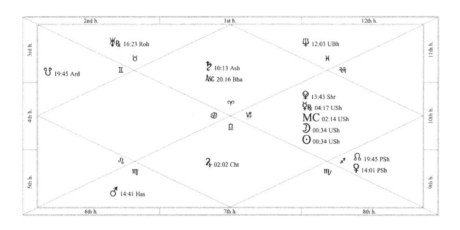

Chart 2 (South Indian diamond style)

- 2nd h.: ♅℞ 16:23 Roh (♉)
- 1st h.: ♄ 10:13 Ash / ASC 20:16 Bha (♈)
- 12th h.: ♆ 12:03 UBh (ℋ)
- 3rd h.: ☊ 19:45 Ard (♊)
- 11th h. (♒)
- 10th h.: ♀ 13:43 Shr / ☿℞ 04:17 USh / MC 02:14 USh / ☽ 00:34 USh / ☉ 00:34 USh
- 4th h. (♋ / ♎ / ♈ / ♑)
- 9th h.: ☋ 19:45 PSh / ♀ 14:01 PSh
- 5th h. (♌ / ♍)
- 6th h.: ♂ 14:41 Has
- 7th h.: ♃ 02:02 Cht
- 8th h.

Chart 3

3rd h.	4th h.	5th h.	6th h.
♆ 16:35 UBh (ℋ)	♄ 25:00 Bha (♈)	☿ 03:53 Kri / ♅ 20:29 Roh / ☽ 27:12 Mrg / ☉ 27:12 Mrg (♉)	☊ 10:23 Ard / ♀ 18:06 Ard (♊)

2nd h.			7th h.
(♒)	June Solar Eclipse 29		(♋)
	Mon 06-11-2029		
(♑)	23:49:57		(♌)
1st h.	Washington, District of Columbia		8th h.
ASC 20:50 Shr / ♀℞ 15:57 Shr	USA		
	Timezone: 5 DST: 1		
	Latitude: 38N53'42		
	Longitude: 77W02'11		
	Ayanamsha : -24:16:23 Lahiri		

12th h.	11th h.	10th h.	9th h.
☋ 10:23 Mul (♐)	MC 08:58 Anu (♍)	(♎)	♂ 08:01 UPh / ♃℞ 23:14 Has (♍)

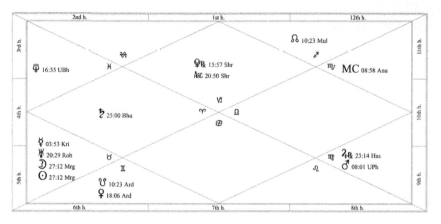

CHAPTER 6

Rahu in Scorpio and Ketu in Taurus

February 04, 2030 to August 9, 2031

This is a time of extremes in weather and earthquakes. Genocide and assassinations were a major part of these planets' positions in the past. Rahu in the sign of Scorpio and Ketu in the sign of Taurus are considered the very worst placements as they are debilitated in these signs. Rahu in the volatile sign of Scorpio can cause violence and emotional outbreaks as well as severity in weather. Ketu in Taurus can indicate extreme desires that may go unfulfilled.

Nakshatras Activated

Rahu in Scorpio (Vishaka, Anuradha, Jyeshta) and Ketu in Taurus (Krittika, Rohini, Mrigashira).

What happened before:

Rahu was in Scorpio and Ketu in Taurus on September 8, 1900. This was one of the deadliest events in USA history where 6,000-12,000 people died in Galveston, Texas, due to the worst hurricane to ever hit the USA.

Jupiter was tightly conjunct Rahu with Uranus in Scorpio, and Pluto with Ketu. Jupiter will magnify the results of Uranus, which is often involved in unexpected and tragic events. During that era, storms of this magnitude were not foreseen by contemporary weather forecasting technology.

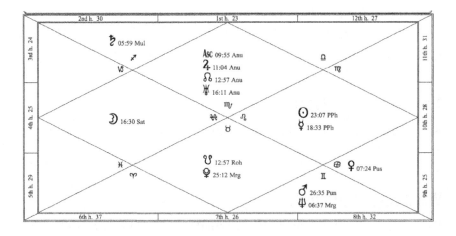

7th h.		8th h.		9th h.		10th h.	
♓		♈		♉		♊	
	♂ 15:39 Bha ♄ 17:54 Bha ♅ 23:45 Bha ♃ 26:10 Bha		♀ 03:26 Kri ♀ 06:34 Kri ☊ 25:44 Mrg			MC 17:47 Ard ☉ 18:40 Ard	

James Garfield shot
Sat 07-02-1881
12:00:00
Washington, District of Columbia
USA
Timezone: 5:08:09 DST: 0
Latitude: 38N53'42
Longitude: 77W02'11
Ayanamsha : -22:12:25 Lahiri

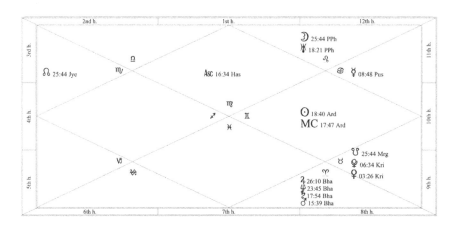

On July 2, 1881, President Garfield became the second president to be shot. Walking through Washington, D.C.'s Baltimore & Potomac train station, President Garfield was shot by Charles Guiteau, a man who had hoped to work for the President. Garfield suffered two gunshots on July 2, 1881, but did not die until 80 days later of complications from sepsis. He might have survived had his injuries not been contaminated, either by the gunshots themselves or the interventions that followed.

Ketu was in Taurus aligned with Pluto which can be great loss and death. Rahu in Scorpio was in the nakshatra Jyestha which can deal with revenge. The assassin apparently was emotionally disturbed in this way.

Also, during this time Mars and Saturn were conjunct indicating attacks and violence Saturn being in its sign of debilitation can indicate violence along with Mars, while it is extremely strong in its own sign of rulership Aries. This combination represents violence and anger. But the most important aspect that reveals the situation is Neptune conjunct Jupiter, which deals with deception, and illusions. These four planets together in Aries represent a violent act that come unexpectedly.

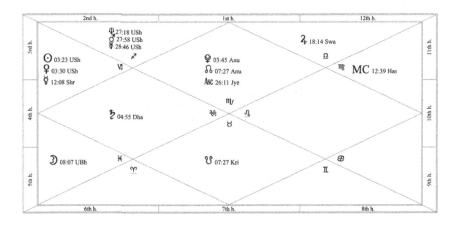

The Northridge Earthquake caused at least 57 fatalities and injured thousands. The earthquake caused upwards of $20 billion in damages, plus $40+ billion in economic loss, making this the costliest earthquake disaster in USA history.

Rahu is conjunct Pluto indicating a difficult time that relates to tragic events. But the most important transits are that the two planets that indicate earthquakes, Neptune and Uranus are both tightly conjunct Mars. Since Rahu is aligned with Pluto for the entire year and a half that Rahu is in Scorpio the triggering of the timing of the event was when Mars aligned with Neptune and Uranus.

Spindletop Oil Field, 1901

January 10, 1901 is the most famous date in Texas petroleum history. This is the date that the great gusher erupted in the oil well being drilled at Spindletop, near Beaumont Texas by a mining engineer, Captain A. F. Lucas.

This was the first salt dome oil discovery where thousands of barrels of oil flowed before the well could be capped. Spindletop created a sensation throughout the world and encouraged exploration and drilling in Texas that has continued to this day.

This timeframe was fascinating since Rahu was conjunct Uranus in Scorpio and Ketu was in Taurus with Pluto. At the time of the gusher erupted Uranus and Pluto were exactly oppose each other. This indicates enormous wealth and expansion. This changed the finances in Texas forever bringing great wealth to this state. When the nodal axis is in Taurus and Scorpio it represents great wealth.

Saturn was opposed Neptune and both these planets rule oil. Saturn rules crude oil and what is beneath the ground, while Neptune rules oil and natural gas. They will always be in aspect of each other when there are major events involving oil.

The Exxon Valdez oil spill was a major environmental disaster that occurred on March 24, 1989, when the oil tanker Exxon Valdez ran aground on Bligh Reef in Alaska's Prince William Sound. The spill released approximately 11 million gallons of crude oil. It affected over 1,300 miles of shoreline and contaminated many areas, including a National Forest, National Wildlife Refuges, National Parks, State Parks, and a State Game Sanctuary.

This chart does not have Rahu in Scorpio or Ketu in Taurus, but It has Saturn and Neptune conjunct within one degree.

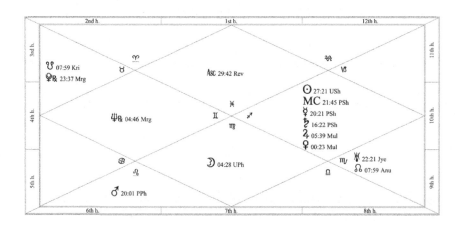

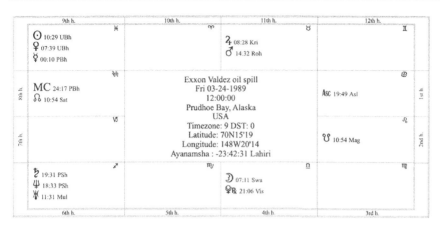

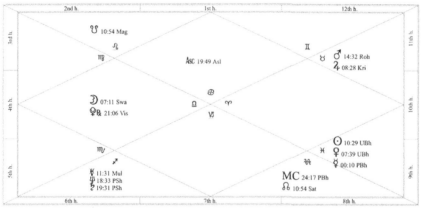

Overall, this is a time for great inventions and discoveries with the advent of the iPhone, putting a man on the Moon for the first time and the Invention of the Internet. These discoveries will again pertain to travel into space as well as technology with air travel. There will be great strides and accomplishments in health and healing of very difficult diseases, and this will also promote longevity for mankind.

The World Wide Web announced that it was for everybody on April 30, 1993, the European Organization for Nuclear Research (CERN) put the web into the public domain—a decision that has fundamentally altered all our lives. During this time, the most significant aspect is the Uranus and Neptune conjunction which only occurs roughly every 165-171 years. Uranus rules technology and Neptune is ethereal. Together these two planets manifested all the technological advancements that changed our world dramatically. The internet, advanced computers and cell phones are a part of this conjunction that was forming throughout the 1990s. But their exact conjunction was 1993 representing the most powerful advancements in technology that transformed all or lives.

Rahu in Scorpio was conjunct Pluto indicating a time of transformation and change. But none of this could have occurred without the Neptune and Uranus conjunction. Rahu in Scorpio and Ketu in Taurus has always indicated expansion and changes with money, finances, and the economy.

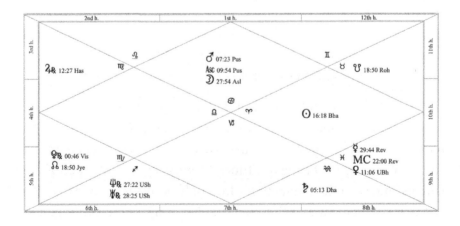

The American Civil War is considered the war with the most lives lost in American history, with an estimated 620,000 fatalities, representing a significant percentage of the population at the time. The most important aspect is Uranus exactly conjunct Ketu when the war began. Uranus is the planet of sudden unexpected strikes and rebellion.

The Jupiter and Saturn conjunction in earth signs aspecting Ketu usually indicates economic expansion but Neptune with retrograde Mars oppose this conjunction reversed gains in the economy. Rahu in Scorpio and Ketu in Taurus indicate extremes in the economy and the financial world changes dramatically during these times.

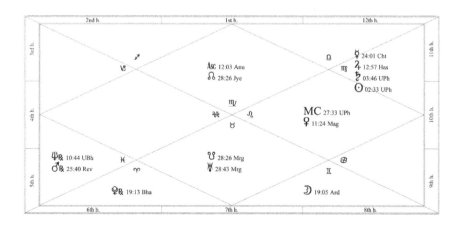

Economic expansions are associated with Jupiter in a trine aspect with Rahu or Ketu, especially in earth signs. Rahu in Scorpio and Ketu in Taurus always indicate extremes in the financial world. It has been a great indicator for an expansive economy but during the time of the Civil War it was the opposite extreme. But during the early 1990s Uranus was conjunct Neptune which prompted the new age of computers and cell phones.

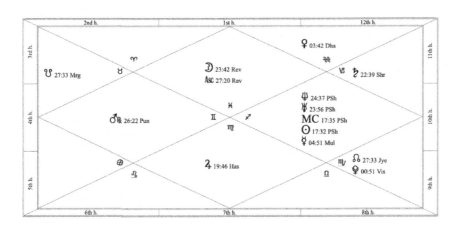

Catastrophic Events with Rahu in Scorpio and Ketu in Taurus

- Bhopal gas tragedy, a chemical leak killed thousands in Bhopal India, December 3, 1984, killed 150,000 – 220,000 people.
- Shri Lankan civil war, civil war between government and Tamil insurgents July 23, 1983, killed 80,000-100,000 people.
- Texas disaster, ship explosion in Texas City April 16, 1947, killed 581 people.
- Superstorm Sandy, arm impacted East Coast of the USA October 29, 2012, killed 233 people.
- Rwandan genocide, genocide in Rwanda targeting the Tulsi population, April 7, 1994, killed 800,000 people.
- Vietnam War, conflict in Vietnam November 1, 1955, killed 3.8 million people.
- Hindenburg disaster, airship Hindenburg caught fire and was destroyed May 6, 1937, killed 36 people.

Predictions for February 04, 2030 to August 9, 2031 : Rahu in Scorpio and Ketu in Taurus

Predictions 2030

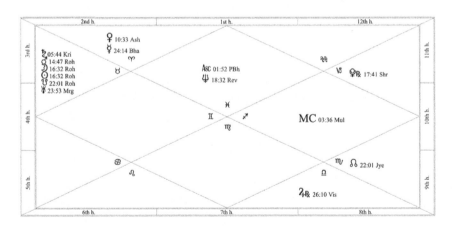

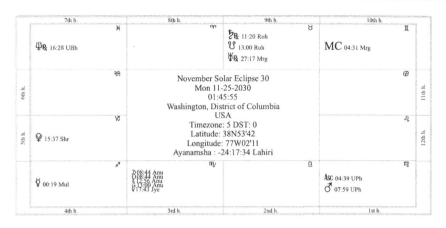

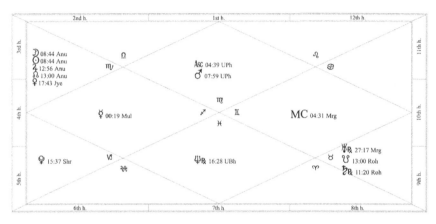

This looks critical and very intense! The chart I use for World War II has Ketu conjunct Saturn and Uranus, but they were in Aries (the chart is displayed in the next segment on Aries/Libra). This time, we have Jupiter and Saturn opposed in Taurus/Scorpio. This is extremely rare and indicates something massive occurring. The last time there was a configuration like this was 263 AD, where Rahu was in Scorpio opposed Ketu, Saturn, and Uranus in Taurus. This was when the Roman Empire split into East and West.

Both signs of Taurus and Scorpio indicate finances and money. Jupiter with Rahu means Jupiter is eclipsed. Jupiter represents finances and the economy. The opposition of Jupiter and Saturn are incredibly meaningful and indicate there is something that is coming to an end. Transiting Saturn conjunct Ketu is always very difficult and represents extreme losses. It is believed in the Vedic text that when transiting Saturn goes into the nakshatra Rohini there is always a devastating event. The last time that Saturn was in Rohini was around September 11, 2001. In the past there were many times that these placements indicated gains and extremes in the economy but this time it looks like there is an explosive event that will shift it to a downward cycle.

Furthermore, Uranus, the planet of unexpected change and disruption, is tied up with Ketu. This means incredible and devastating changes that will hit the planet unexpectedly. It is almost like an asteroid or something unknown will strike out of the blue and disrupts our planet, or it can mean a major nuclear strike.

June 1, 2030, during the solar eclipse, Uranus will be at 23° of Taurus which is a critical degree as Jupiter was on this degree during the Tiananmen Square massacre and the bombing of Pearl Harbor.

Most importantly, Uranus was at this degree, 23° Taurus at the time of the nuclear bombing of Hiroshima.

In this instance Uranus and Ketu are aligned at this sensitive degree point that has continually depicted catastrophic events.

Both eclipses this year indicate great danger, losses, turbulence, and unexpected catastrophic events. This will of course throw the economy into complete disarray, causing a depression.

Meanwhile transiting Pluto sits at 15° of Capricorn, which is conjunct Ketu in the USA chart in the 2nd house of finances and money. Therefore, transiting Pluto is tied up with the nodal axis of the USA chart indicating extremes in financial gains and extreme losses with corruption being exposed. Since Scorpio pertains to jealousy and revenge it appears that there will be unrelenting revenge and attacks towards the USA.

During the November solar eclipse Neptune is opposed Mars, which also indicates extreme deception, illusions, disease, but most of all something's coming out that was totally unseen and hidden. It could pertain to biological warfare. There will be secret agendas and attacks around the world, which could indicate a World War.

Predictions 2031

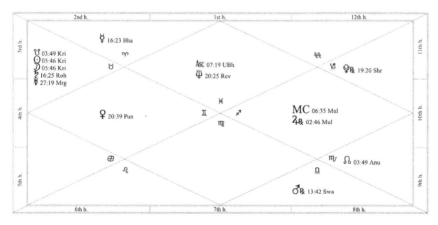

For the first part of the year until August 9, 2031, Ketu will be in Taurus and Rahu will be in Scorpio. This extends the dire effects of Saturn being conjunct Uranus and Ketu. Saturn combined with the destructive unexpected energy of Uranus indicates mystery and unseen obstacles. New unforeseen problems surface and develop.

Half of the year Jupiter will spend time in Scorpio and the other half of the year in Sagittarius. Jupiter will be in Sagittarius from February 17, 2031 to June 13, 2031 and then again October 15, 2031 it returns to Sagittarius. During the time that Jupiter is in Scorpio, it is in opposition to both Saturn and Uranus causing extreme events throughout the world.

January 4, 2031, Mars enters Libra and remains there due to its retrograde cycle until August 15, 2031. While Mars is retrograde in Libra, it will be aspecting with its full 8th aspect to all the planets in Taurus during this time. This means Mars aspects Ketu, Saturn, and Uranus. It appears one major catastrophe after another occurs during this time. By the time Mars is about to leave Libra on August 14, 2031 it will exactly conjunct Rahu at 29° of Libra, as Rahu has just shifted into the sign of Libra. This denotes great violence and upsets, indicating problems around war and attacks.

Another issue that is occurring at this time is that Saturn will be in the nakshatra Rohini, which has been mentioned throughout the Vedic texts as being the worst place for transiting Saturn. As I mentioned before during September 11, 2001 when the world trade center in New York was attacked by terrorists, transiting Saturn was in Rohini.

Another enormous change for this year is that transiting Uranus will shift signs from Taurus into Gemini on July 5, 2031. It will remain there until it retrogrades back into Taurus January 8, 2032, but will finally return to stay in Gemini by April 20, 2032. As Uranus transits into the sign of Gemini it will be crossing over four very important planets in the chart for the USA. Most importantly in the chart for the USA, natal

Mars sits at 0° of Gemini. Every time Uranus transits into this sign it will be conjunct Mars, which represents unforeseen, unexpected, sudden violence. It appears the world is at odds and constantly at war, this looks like an ongoing World War III.

On a good note, transiting Uranus was in Gemini from 1948 to 1955, which was a time of healing from the ravages of World War II. So hopefully, this indicates a healing from the effects of this year.

CHAPTER 7

Rahu in Libra and Ketu in Aries

August 9, 2031 to January 29, 2033

The Assassinations of President Lincoln and President McKinley and World War II began indicating a time of social unrest and destruction. Severe weather dominates with Rahu in an air sign. New discoveries played out with Columbus discovering America. Overall, it was a disastrous time!

Nakshatras Activated

Rahu in Libra (Chitra, Swati, Vishaka) and Ketu in Aries (Ashwini, Bharani, Krittika).

What happened before:

Malaysian flight MH370 disappeared without a trace into the Indian Ocean. To this day no one knows for sure what happened. Rahu was in Libra (conjunct Saturn and Mars) and Ketu was in Aries. Rahu in air signs often indicates problems with air travel.

The weather seems to be bitter cold when Saturn is conjunct Rahu in Swati, a very cold and airy nakshatra.

Columbus discovered America in 1492 when Rahu was in Libra and Ketu in Aries. With Ketu in the sign of pioneers and new discoveries, the Europeans finally discovered America.

President Lincoln was assassinated April 14, 1865, when Saturn and Rahu were in Libra. Saturn conjunct Rahu generally portrays extreme and violent events.

Another assassination occurred with a USA President, William McKinley in 1901.

World War II started September 1, 1939, while Rahu was in Libra (Swati) and Ketu was in Aries (Ashwini). This was the beginning of one of the most violent and disastrous periods in history. These nakshatras are ruled by Rahu and Ketu, Ashwini is ruled by Ketu and Swati is ruled by Rahu. This indicates these nakshatras are extreme and indicate fated events.

What surfaces during eclipses in these signs is the seething anger that causes the world to explode with violence.

When Rahu is in an air sign there's often very bad weather and earth changes. Based on the previous events of these placements of the nodes this is one of the most intense periods of all. There appears to be extreme violence as in World War II and two presidential assassinations and problems with air travel with the Malaysian flight.

5th h. 30	6th h. 29	7th h. 28	8th h. 27
⛢ 16:58 Rev	☋ 05:11 Ash	☽ 13:14 Roh	♃ 16:23 Ard
☉ 22:58 PBh ♆ 11:26 Sat	Malaysian Flight 370 Sat 03-08-2014 00:41:00 Kuala Lumpor, Kuala Lumpur		
☿ 26:31 Dha ♀ 07:28 USh	Malaysia Timezone: -8 DST: 0 Latitude: 03N10'00 Longitude: 101E42'00 Ayanamsha : -24:03:28 Lahiri		
♀ 19:08 PSh	ASC 13:44 Anu	♂℞ 03:14 Cht ☊ 05:11 Cht ♄℞ 29:14 Vis	
2nd h. 27	1st h. 36	12th h. 27	11th h. 28

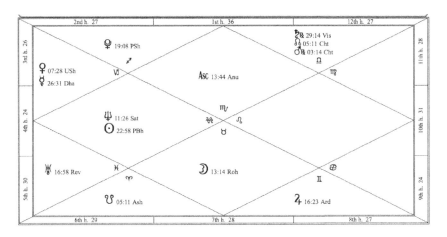

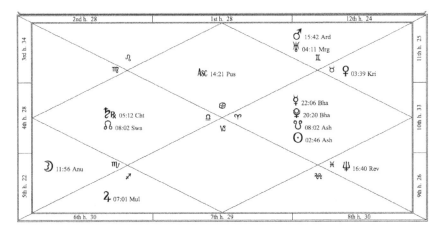

5th h. 23	6th h. 29	7th h. 27	8th h. 29
☽ 15:50 UBh ♃℞ 13:57 UBh	☋ 07:19 Ash ♄℞ 07:57 Aah ♅℞ 28:56 Kri	World War II Fri 09-01-1939 12:00:00	
4th h. 29		Washington, District of Columbia USA	♀ 09:04 Pus ☿ 28:06 Asl 9th h. 23
3rd h. 35 ♂ 01:25 USh		Timezone: 5 DST: 0 Latitude: 38N53'42 Longitude: 77W02'11 Ayanamsha : -23:01:02 Lahiri	♀ 14:11 PPh ☉ 15:19 PPh ♆ 29:29 UPh 10th h. 29
2nd h. 28	ASC 01:17 Vis 1st h. 32	☊ 07:19 Swa 12th h. 24	11th h. 29

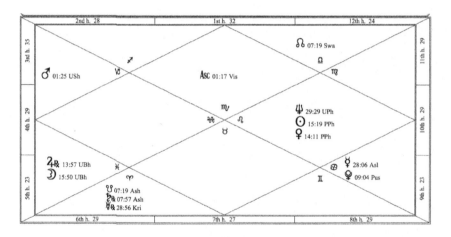

4th h. 30	5th h. 31	6th h. 38	7th h. 24
	☋ 17:56 Bha		
3rd h. 24	Columbus Discovered America Fri 10-12-1492 12:00:00		☽ 04:17 Pus ♃ 23:24 Asl 8th h. 25
2nd h. 24 ♄ 26:47 Dha ♅ 07:14 USh	New York, New York USA Timezone: 4:56:01 DST: 0 Latitude: 40N42'51 Longitude: 74W00'22 Ayanamsha : -16:46:56 Lahiri	♂ 12:08 Mag	9th h. 29
ASC 21:16 PSh ♆ 10:35 Mul 1st h. 25	♀℞ 00:28 Vis ☿ 03:46 Anu 12th h. 24	☉ 11:57 Swa ☊ 17:56 Swa ♀ 27:17 Vis 11th h. 27	10th h. 36

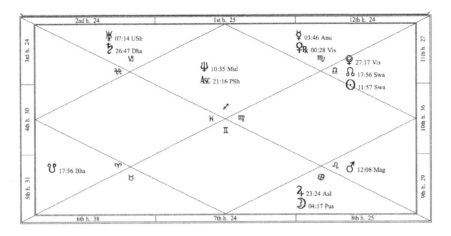

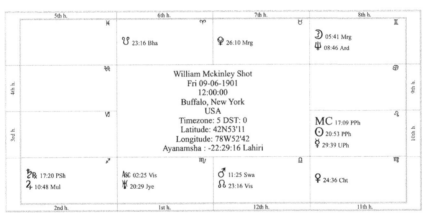

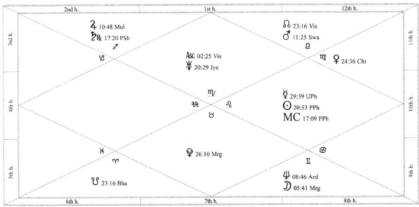

Catastrophic Events Rahu in Libra and Ketu in Aries

- Krakatoa eruption, massive eruption in Indonesia August 27, 1883, killing 36,000 people.
- Mount Pelee eruption, volcanic eruption in Martinique May 8, 1902, killing 30 people.
- World War 2, global war involving most nations September 1, 1939, killing 70-85 million people.
- Tang Shan earthquake July 28, 1976, killing 242,000 people.
- Guatemala earthquake February 4, 1976, killing 23,000 people.
- Oklahoma City bombing, domestic terrorist attack in Oklahoma April 19, 1995, killing 168 people.
- Kobe, Japan earthquake January 17, 1995, killing 6,434 people.
- Super Typhoon Haiyan (known locally as Yolanda) in the Philippines November 8, 2013 killed 6,300 people.
- Lushan earthquake in Sichuan China April 20, 2013, killing 196 people.
- Ebola outbreak March 23, 2014, killing 325 people.

Future Predictions August 9, 2031 – January 29, 2033 : Rahu in Libra and Ketu in Aries

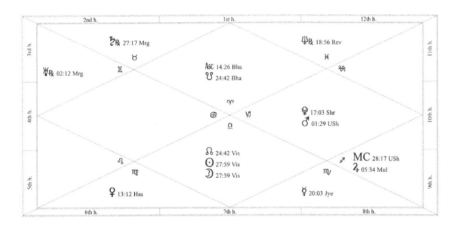

North Indian chart:

12th h.	1st h.	2nd h.	3rd h.
♆℞ 18:56 Rev	ASC 14:26 Bha ☋ 24:42 Bha	♄℞ 27:17 Mrg	♅℞ 02:12 Mrg

November Solar Eclipse 31
Fri 11-14-2031
16:10:39
Washington, District of Columbia
USA
Timezone: 5 DST: 0
Latitude: 38N53'42
Longitude: 77W02'11
Ayanamsha : -24:18:20 Lahiri

11th h.			4th h.
♀ 17:03 Shr ♂ 01:29 USh (10th)			5th h.
MC 28:17 USh ♃ 05:34 Mul (9th h.)	☿ 20:03 Jye (8th h.)	☊ 24:42 Vis ☉ 27:59 Vis ☽ 27:59 Vis (7th h.)	♀ 13:12 Has (6th h.)

South Indian chart:

2nd h.		1st h.	12th h.
♄℞ 27:17 Mrg		ASC 14:26 Bha ☋ 24:42 Bha	♆℞ 18:56 Rev
♅℞ 02:12 Mrg (3rd h.)			♀ 17:03 Shr ♂ 01:29 USh (11th h.)
(4th h.)			(10th h.)
♀ 13:12 Has (5th h.)	☊ 24:42 Vis ☉ 27:59 Vis ☽ 27:59 Vis (6th h.)	☿ 20:03 Jye (7th h.)	MC 28:17 USh ♃ 05:34 Mul (9th h. / 8th h.)

Rahu and Ketu in these explosive signs will continue with war and fighting. Particularly since Uranus enters the air sign of Gemini activating the planets in the birth chart for the USA. One positive aspect is that transiting Jupiter will be in Sagittarius aspecting Uranus in Gemini. This indicates new discoveries in air travel. Remember, Christopher Columbus discovered America with Rahu in Libra and Ketu in Aries. Aries is the sign of pioneers. This could also motivate space travel in many new progressive ways. Possibly using other means of fuel or propulsion which could revolutionize the way we travel.

Jupiter in the sign of Sagittarius will promote healing, spirituality, and justice for all. It will be casting an aspect to Ketu activating the desire to heal the planet. There will be more hope and inspiration to move on from aggression and violence. Jupiter will be in Sagittarius from February 17, 2031 to June 13, 2031, then again October 15, 2031 to March 5, 2032.

Predictions 2032

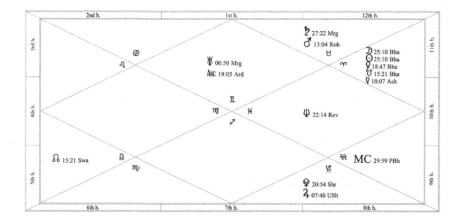

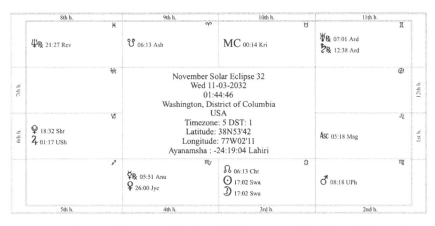

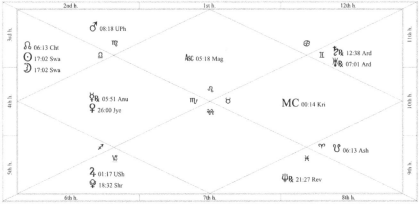

April 20, 2032, Uranus will transit into Gemini and will transit over natal Mars in the USA chart. This will cause disruption, uneasiness, and sudden unexpected events particularly around air travel. This could then indicate some type of new discoveries in air travel and technology.

May 30, 2032, Saturn will enter Gemini, and this again will cross over Natal Mars in the USA chart. This can indicate sudden setbacks and delays concerning inventions and futuristic discoveries. On June 28, 2032, Saturn will conjunct Uranus around 3 to 4° of Gemini. This conjunction has previously indicated war and violence. Futuristic and progressive projects are on their way but seem to be temporarily delayed by unexpected events.

Transiting Mars will conjunct Uranus June 7, 2032, at 2° of Gemini. This activates futuristic inventions in technology, especially air travel and space travel. There is an incredible leap in all technologies this year. Technological advances seem to come from unforeseen places, possibly information from other worlds or aliens.

Transiting Jupiter will be in the sign of Capricorn for most of 2032. Jupiter will spend six weeks in the sign of Sagittarius from August 12, 2032 to October 23, 2032. While Jupiter is in its sign of debilitation, Capricorn and it is in the difficult 8 and 6 spacial relationship known as a quincunx, and aspects Saturn. This means that this is not a great year for the economy and or the stock market.

November 23, 2032, Mars will oppose Neptune from Virgo to Pisces. This can indicate problems in health and disease during this time. There can be great deception occurring within the world's governments. Corruption and hidden agendas are a possibility in an effort to level out the world population.

CHAPTER 8

Rahu in Virgo and Ketu in Pisces

January 29, 2033 to August 12, 2034

Mass suicides and controls through cults, terrorist attacks, with the emphasis on deception and delusions.

Nakshatras Activated

Rahu in Virgo (Uttara Phalguni, Hasta, Chitra) and Ketu in Pisces (Purva Bhadrapada, Uttara Bhadrapada).

What happened before:

During the Paris attacks on November 13, 2015, at least 128 people were killed in gunfire and blasts during a concert in the Bataclan night club. Rahu was in Virgo with Mars. This alerted the world to the terror taking place all over Europe, and the specter of more to come. The birth charts of the countries under attack are connected. In the chart for France, Rahu is in Virgo and Ketu is in Pisces.

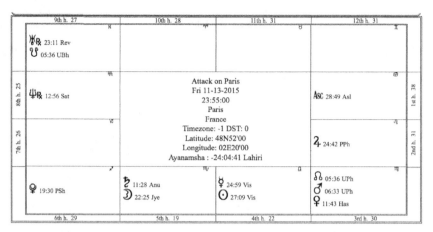

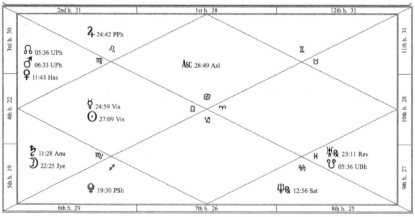

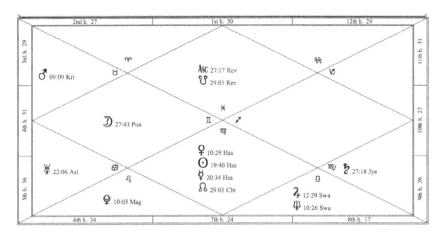

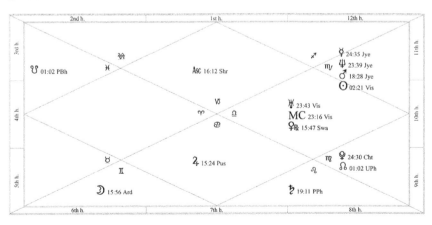

In November 1978, the world was shocked by the mass murder-suicide of more than 900 members of the California-based Peoples Temple cult. Members of its Jonestown commune in Guyana drank cyanide-laced fruit drink after being ordered to do so by their cult leader, Jim Jones.

Though the Peoples Temple presented itself as humanitarian organization, members of the church were not treated humanely. They were often blackmailed, humiliated, and beaten. Many were brainwashed or coerced into signing over their homes and possessions to Jim Jones and the church. Black members of the church were convinced by Jones that they would be sent to concentration camps if they ever left.

When members of the press began asking questions in 1977, Jim Jones moved hundreds of his congregation to South America to Jonestown, a compound in Guyana.

Jones ordered a "revolutionary suicide" at the compound. A fruit drink laced with sedatives, tranquilizers, and cyanide was handed out, first given to babies and children, and then ingested by the adult members. In all, 918 people died that day, 304 of them under the age of 18. Jones himself died of a gunshot wound. Fewer than 100 of the Temple members in Guyana survived the massacre.

10th h.		11th h.	12th h.		1st h.
♄26:54 Rev ♂16:55 UBh MC 13:57 UBh ☿ 12:57 UBh ☉ 16:40 UBh ♀ 04:54 UBh	♓	♈		♉	♊
					ASC 26:36 Pun
9th h.	♒	Heaven's Gate Wed 03-26-1997 12:00:00 San Diego, California			♋ 2nd h.
8th h.	♑	USA Timezone: 8 DST: 0 Latitude: 32N42'55 Longitude: 117W09'26 Ayanamsha : -23:49:05 Lahiri		♂R 29:17 UPh	♌ 3rd h.
♃ 20:14 Shr ♆ 13:56 Shr ♇ 05:47 USh					
	♐	♏	♎		♍
	♀R 11:41 Anu	☽ 12:02 Swa	☊ 04:54 UPh		
7th h.		6th h.	5th h.		4th h.

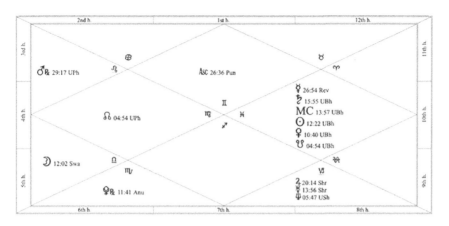

In San Diego California, 39 victims were involved in a mass suicide called Heaven's Gate. Leaders of this cult preached that suicide would allow them to leave their bodily "containers" and enter an alien spacecraft hidden behind the Hale-Bopp comet.

The cult was led by Marshall Applewhite, a music professor who, after surviving a near-death experience in 1972, was recruited into the cult by one of his nurses, Bonnie Lu Nettles. In 1975, Applewhite and Nettles persuaded a group of 20 people from Oregon to abandon their families and possessions and move to eastern Colorado, where they were promised that an extraterrestrial spacecraft would take them to the "kingdom of heaven."

What is amazing is that both cults Jim Jones with Jonestown and Heaven's Gate happened years apart. However, during both these times Ketu was in Pisces, which is the sign of otherworldly spirituality or illusions and cults. Interestingly as well, both cult leaders were born within a few days of each other.

4th h.		5th h.	6th h.		7th h.	
♄ 28:46 Rev ♅ 24:30 Rev ☊ 21:04 Rev ☽ 20:11 Rev	♓	♀ 10:41 Ash ♈ ☉ 29:31 Kri	♉	♃ 24:02 Pun ♀ 26:08 Pun		♊
	♒	**JIM JONES** Wed 05-13-1931 22:21:00		♂ 23:23 Asl		♋
	♑	LYNN, IN,Indiana USA Timezone: 6 DST: 0				♌
♄℞ 00:17 USh		Latitude: 40N02'59 Longitude: 84W56'23 Ayanamsha : -22:53:49 Lahiri		♆℞ 10:05 Mag		
ASC 16:30 PSh	♐	♍	MC 10:35 Swa	♎	☋ 21:04 Has	♏
1st h.		12th h.	11th h.		10th h.	

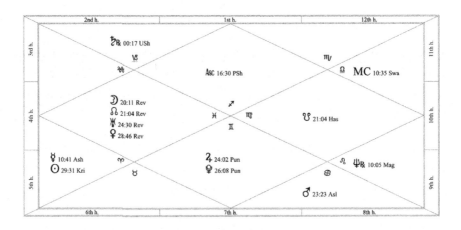

1st h.		2nd h.	3rd h.		4th h.	
♅ 24:39 Rev ☊ 20:55 Rev ASC 12:04 UBh	♓	♀ 02:37 Ash ♈ ☿ 11:13 Ash ☽ 29:36 Kri	☉ 02:36 Kri ♉	♃ 24:35 Pun ♀ 26:11 Pun		♊
	♒	**MARSHALL APPLEWHITE** Sun 05-17-1931 03:20:00		♂ 24:53 Asl		♋
	♑	SPUR, Texas USA Timezone: 6 DST: 0				♌
♄℞ 00:13 USh		Latitude: 33N28'35 Longitude: 100W51'19 Ayanamsha : -22:53:50 Lahiri		♆ 10:05 Mag		
MC 10:05 Mul	♐	♍		♎	☋ 20:55 Has	♍
10th h.		9th h.	8th h.		7th h.	

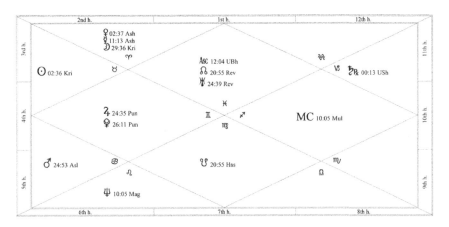

They both had Rahu in Pisces and Ketu in Virgo which is the reversal of where the nodes were transiting at the times of these mass suicides. It was close to 18 to19 years apart when Rahu and Ketu returned to these signs.

Insulin was first used as a treatment for diabetes in 1922. It was discovered the previous year by scientists at the University of Toronto. Before this discovery was made, Type 1 diabetes (typically diagnosed in young people) couldn't be successfully treated.

The life changing discovery of Insulin saved so many lives. Rahu in Virgo and Ketu in Pisces are the indicators of health and healing discoveries. Rahu with Saturn and Jupiter added the enormous power of this incredible live saving discovery.

8th h.		9th h.	10th h.		11th h.	
	♓		♈	♉	☿ 07:24 Ard	♊
☋ 13:44 UBh		MC 29:11 Kri	☉ 17:34 Roh		♀ 15:37 Ard	
					♀ 16:03 Ard	
	♒		Insulin			⊕
♅ 20:42 PBh			Thu 06-01-1922		♆ 20:47 Asl	
7th h.			12:00:00			12th h.
	♑		Tottenham, Ontario			♌
6th h.			Canada		☽ 03:13 Mag	1st h.
			Timezone: 5 DST: 1		Asc 06:17 Mag	
			Latitude: 44N01'00			
			Longitude: 79W48'00			
			Ayanamsha : -22:46:26 Lahiri			
	♐		♍	♎	♄℞ 08:02 UPh	♍
		♂℞ 28:51 Jye			☊ 13:44 Has	
					♃℞ 16:13 Has	
5th h.		4th h.	3rd h.		2nd h	

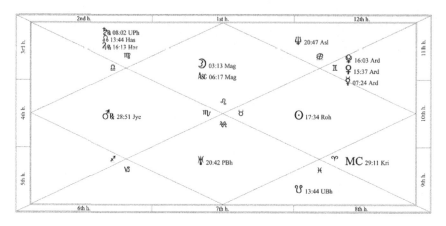

The Wright Flyer also known as the Kitty Hawk, made the first sustained flight by a manned heavier-than-air powered and controlled aircraft, on December 17, 1903. Invented and flown by brothers Orville and Wilbur Wright, it marked the beginning of the pioneer era of aviation.

During this time Rahu was in Virgo and Ketu in Pisces. These signs have indicated invention and new discoveries. But the two outer planets that indicate major change for humanity has always been Uranus and Neptune and they were fully aspecting each other by opposition. These two planets are at the midpoint of Rahu and Ketu. This was the exact combination needed to activate the invention of air travel.

2nd h.		3rd h.	4th h.		5th h.	
	ℋ	♈		♉		♊
☋ 10:41 UBh		♀℞ 27:04 Mrg	♅℞ 12:18 Ard			
	♒	**Airplane Kitty Hawk**				♋
ASC 28:38 PBh		Thu 12-17-1903				
♃ 23:16 PBh		12:00:00				
	♑	Kitty Hawk, North Carolina				♌
♄ 13:59 Shr		USA				
♂ 11:36 Shr		Timezone: 5 DST: 0				
		Latitude: 36N03'53				
		Longitude: 75W42'21				
	♐	Ayanamsha : -22:30:57 Lahiri	♍	♎		♍
☿ 16:18 PSh						
♆ 03:13 Mul		☽ 18:26 Jye	♀ 16:22 Swa	☊ 10:41 Has		
MC 02:22 Mul						
☉ 02:04 Mul						
11th h.		10th h.	9th h.		8th h.	

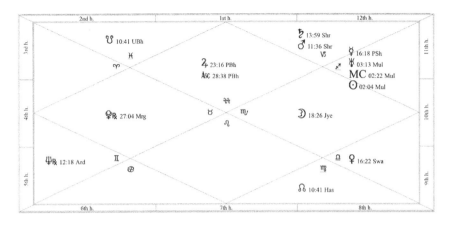

Catastrophic Events Rahu in Virgo and Ketu in Pisces

- Yellowstone earthquake August 17, 1959, 28 people killed.
- Nepal earthquake April 25, 2015, 8,964 people killed.
- Yemen civil war March 19, 2015, 250,000 people killed.

It appears that the main events during this time involved illusionary deceptions. The attack in Paris was a violent terrorist attack and involved transiting Mars with Rahu, as Mars with Rahu indicates violence. It must be noted that France could have another attack or major problems with terrorism when Rahu is in Virgo and Ketu in Pisces.

Predictions for Rahu in Virgo and Ketu in Pisces – January 29, 2033 to August 12, 2034

Predictions for 2033

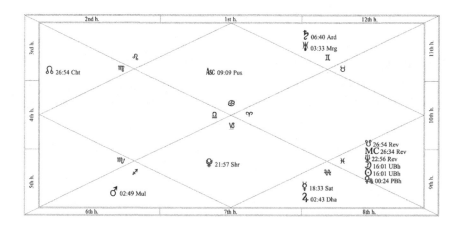

9th h.		10th h.		11th h.		12th h.	
☊ 26:54 Rev ⚷ 26:34 Rev ♇ 22:56 Rev ☽ 16:01 UBh ♆ 00:24 PBh	♓		♈		♉	♅ 03:33 Mrg ♄ 06:40 Ard	♊
☿ 18:33 Sat ♃ 02:43 Dha	♒	March Solar Eclipse 33 Wed 03-30-2033 13:51:37 Washington, District of Columbia USA Timezone: 5 DST: 1 Latitude: 38N53'42 Longitude: 77W02'11 Ayanamsha : -24:19:23 Lahiri				ASC 09:09 Pus	♋
♀ 21:57 Shr	♑						♌
♂ 02:49 Mul	♐		♏		♎	☋ 26:54 Cht	♍
6th h.		5th h.		4th h.		3rd h.	

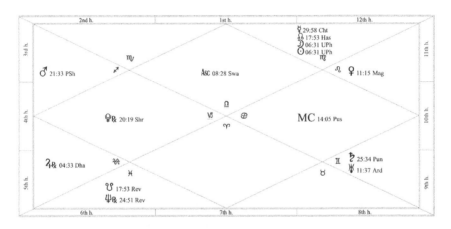

This year transiting Jupiter will be in the sign of Aquarius from March 17, 2033, through March 27, 2034. Jupiter in the sign of Aquarius represents a quest for humanity in a push towards healing in health and environmental matters. When Ketu enters Pisces January 29, 2033, Ketu will be gandanta at the last degree of a water sign at 29° of Pisces. This indicates severe weather, storms, and out-of-control behavior shaking things up on a global level.

February 2, 2033, Jupiter will conjunct Pluto and the Sun exactly at 20° of Capricorn. This denotes great power in leadership since Jupiter is debilitated in Capricorn. It represents difficulties in the economy, especially since it is in a quincunx aspect with Saturn. A major shift will occur financially in areas such as the stock market, as Jupiter goes into Aquarius and aligns in a trine aspect with Saturn. Jupiter in Capricorn quincunx Saturn can represent economic struggles, but the trine of Rahu to Jupiter indicates expansion and gains. The economy will be up and down. There will be indications of positive trends throughout the time that Jupiter transits in Capricorn.

June 10, 2033, Ketu will conjunct Neptune exactly at 25° Pisces. This indicates deception, illusion, and scandals. I believe it can be indicative of many cults that are involved in mind control. People are searching for a way to escape problems and difficulties in their lives. Since Rahu is in Virgo the sign pertaining to health and healing there may be many problems in the health field especially around mental disease.

Mars will be retrograde from May 26, 2033 to August 1, 2033, and remain in the sign of Sagittarius from March 24, 2033 to October 8, 2033. Mars can be very empowering in the sign of Sagittarius, but it will be opposed Saturn throughout the time frame that it is in Sagittarius because Saturn is in Gemini. Mars opposite Saturn can cause all sorts of setbacks, delays, and difficulties because they are in both signs that pertain to travel – Sagittarius and Gemini. There will be major disruptions in air travel throughout this time that Mars is retrograde. Mars will oppose Saturn exactly three times, April 10, 2033 at 7° Sagittarius/Gemini, again June 19, 2033 at 14° Sagittarius/Gemini, and lastly September 30, 2033 at 25° Sagittarius/Gemini. Each of these oppositions will intensify the setbacks and problems concerning travel as well as communications. This may mean there will be power outages, computer shut downs, and major issues dealing with technology during this time.

The entire time that Mars is opposing Saturn, it is also opposing Uranus as Uranus is transiting very close to Saturn throughout this year. From the beginning of the year 2033 through April 2033, Saturn and Uranus will be within a 3° orb indicating again, issues concerning computers and communications in technology. This may be a major cycle for extreme power outages and technological failures, which may be because of communication warfare.

Predictions 2034

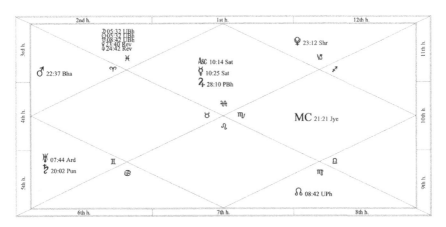

Rahu is in Virgo and Ketu is in Pisces until August 12, 2034. As Ketu is in the earlier degrees of Pisces this can cause great storms and severe weather especially since the March solar eclipse will occur on the fixed star Scheat, which deals with tragedy particularly concerning the oceans and the seas.

Uranus will be at the midpoint of Rahu and Ketu indicating a time of sudden unexpected events, especially casualties caused from earthquakes or unexpected sudden changes with severe weather.

There will be remarkable developments concerning inventions that connect people, especially through travel, as the era of aviation came into the world in 1903 with the airplane when Ketu was in Pisces. Pisces is a sign of travel beyond this world. In 1922 Insulin was used as a treatment for diabetes when Rahu was in Virgo the sign of health and healing.

CHAPTER 9

Rahu in Leo and Ketu in Aquarius

August 12, 2034 to April 12, 2036

From past historical events, Rahu in Leo and Ketu and Aquarius has produced some of the strongest earthquakes ever recorded in history. The other events that occurred during these times involved deception and scandals which involved the media. Another moment in history with Rahu in Leo and Ketu in Aquarius was the unexpected attack on America that began the involvement of the USA in World War II.

Nakshatras Activated

Rahu in Leo (Magha, Purva Phalguni, Uttara Phalguni) and Ketu in Aquarius (Dhanishta, Shatabhishak, Purva Bhadrapada).

What happened before:

The Japanese surprise attack on Pearl Harbor, December 7, 1941, precipitated the entry of the USA into World War II. Since Leo indicates leadership, control, and taking charge, the presence of Rahu in Leo, Ketu in Aquarius, can indicate fighting back. It can also be the emergence of events pertaining to controversy or war.

During the 2016 USA Presidential elections, the media tried to influence the election results. This was due to the eclipses falling in Leo and Aquarius, involving Neptune's deception, deceit, and dishonesty, which could have been said about every politician in the world at this time.

There was corruption in Turkey, South and North Korea, Malaysia, Brazil, China, France, and the USA, to name just a few. An attempted coup in Turkey took the country by surprise in July 2016 but the government turned it to their favor.

Rahu was in Leo, Ketu in Aquarius with Neptune, from January 2016 to September 2017.

In 1997-1998 there was a scandal involving Monica Lewinsky and President Clinton. President Clinton was impeached and charged with perjury but was acquitted of the charges. Rahu was in Leo, Ketu in Aquarius. Scandalous affairs seem to surface when the nodes are transiting these signs. Jupiter was conjunct Ketu in Shatabhishak.

The eclipses in Leo and Aquarius revealed truth, but many chose not to see it. There is great effort to cover up facts. But the truth will surface as it did with the Clintons both times, 1998 and 2016.

The death of Princess Diana occurred August 31, 1997, when Rahu was in Leo and Ketu in Aquarius. Many conspiracy theorists believed this was no accident.

On May 22, 1960, a Magnitude 9.5 earthquake, the largest earthquake ever instrumentally recorded, occurred off the coast of southern Chile. This earthquake generated a tsunami that was destructive not only along the coast of Chile, but also across the Pacific in Hawaii, Japan, and the Philippines.

Chart 1

2nd h. 33	3rd h. 30	4th h. 29	5th h. 21

♂ 22:33 Rev

♄R 00:26 Kri
⛢R 04:35 Kri
♃R 23:26 Mrg

1st h. 25 — ☋ 24:58 PBh, ASC 18:39 Sat
12th h. 26 — ♀ 08:43 USh

Pearl Harbor
Sun 12-07-1941
12:00:00
Honolulu, Hawaii
USA
Timezone: 10:30:00 DST: 0
Latitude: 21N18'25
Longitude: 157W51'30
Ayanamsha : -23:02:41 Lahiri

6th h. 26 — ☽ 07:21 Pus, ♀R 12:31 Pus
7th h. 26 — ☊ 24:58 PPh

☿ 14:37 Anu
☉ 22:24 Jye

♆ 06:39 UPh

11th h. 33	10th h. 29	9th h. 23	8th h. 36

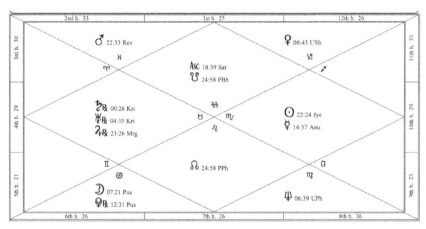

Chart 2 (diamond)

- 2nd h. 33: ♂ 22:33 Rev
- 1st h. 25: ASC 18:39 Sat, ☋ 24:58 PBh
- 12th h. 26: ♀ 08:43 USh
- 3rd h. 30
- 4th h. 29: ♄R 00:26 Kri, ⛢R 04:35 Kri, ♃R 23:26 Mrg
- 10th h. 29: ☉ 22:24 Jye, ☿ 14:37 Anu
- 11th h. 33
- 5th h. 21: ☽ 07:21 Pus, ♀R 12:31 Pus
- 6th h. 26
- 7th h. 26: ☊ 24:58 PPh
- 8th h. 36: ♆ 06:39 UPh
- 9th h. 23

Chart 3

8th h. 26	9th h. 32	10th h. 26	11th h. 27

⛢R 27:27 Rev

7th h. 23 — ☋ 16:08 Sat, ♆R 15:11 Sat, ☽ 09:54 Sat

6th h. 29 — ♂ 05:52 USh

2016 U.S. Elections
Tue 11-08-2016
23:55:00
Washington, District of Columbia
USA
Timezone: 5 DST: 0
Latitude: 38N53'42
Longitude: 77W02'11
Ayanamsha : -24:05:26 Lahiri

12th h. 34
1st h. 35 — ASC 00:12 Mag, ☊ 16:08 PPh

♇ 21:18 PSh
♀ 02:19 Mul

☿ 00:38 Vis
♄ 21:09 Jye

☉ 23:07 Vis

♃ 18:44 Has

5th h. 21	4th h. 28	3rd h. 27	2nd h. 29

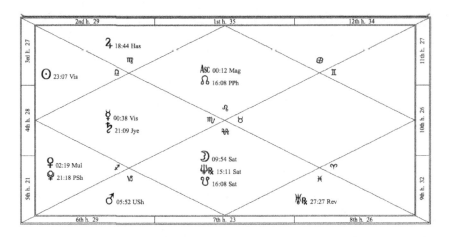

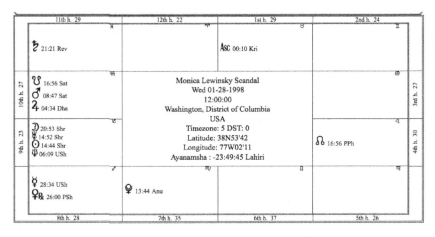

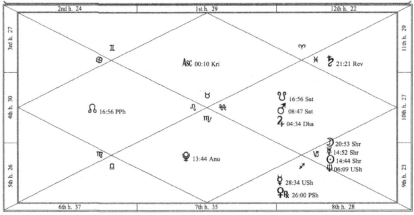

Chart 1 — North Indian style

11th h. 25	12th h. 23	1st h. 37	2nd h. 33
♄℞ 25:49 Rev		ASC 26:28 Mrg	

10th h. 22 — ☋ 25:54 PBh

9th h. 29 — ♃℞ 20:32 Shr / ♅℞ 11:40 Shr / ♆℞ 03:45 USh

Princess Diana Death
Sun 08-31-1997
00:35:00
Paris
France
Timezone: -1 DST: 1
Latitude: 48N52'00
Longitude: 02E20'00
Ayanamsha : -23:49:26 Lahiri

3rd h. 30 — ☽ 21:22 Asl

4th h. 31 — ☉ 13:45 PPh / ☿℞ 14:57 PPh / ☊ 25:54 PPh

8th h. 29	7th h. 27	6th h. 31	5th h. 20
	☿ 09:05 Anu	♂ 16:38 Swa	♀ 21:57 Has

Chart 2 — South Indian style

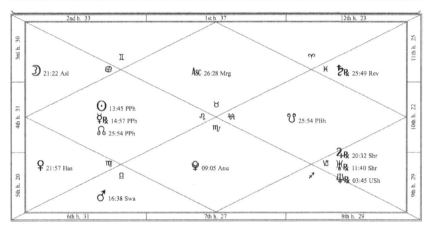

Chart layout:

- 2nd h. 33
- 3rd h. 30: ☽ 21:22 Asl — ⊕ (Gemini ♊)
- 1st h. 37: ASC 26:28 Mrg — (Taurus ♉ / ♌ / ♏ / ♒)
- 12th h. 23: (Aries ♈) ♄℞ 25:49 Rev (Pisces ♓)
- 11th h. 25
- 4th h. 31: ☉ 13:45 PPh / ☿℞ 14:57 PPh / ☊ 25:54 PPh
- 10th h. 22: ☋ 25:54 PBh
- 5th h. 20: ♀ 21:57 Has (♍) / (♎)
- 9th h. 29: ♃℞ 20:32 Shr / ♅℞ 11:40 Shr / ♆℞ 03:45 USh (♑ / ♐)
- 6th h. 31: ♂ 16:38 Swa
- 7th h. 27: ☿ 09:05 Anu
- 8th h. 29

Chart 3 — North Indian style

5th h.	6th h.	7th h.	8th h.
♂ 15:29 UBh	☽ 08:54 Ash	♀ 00:06 Kri / ☉ 08:26 Kri / ☿ 14:51 Roh	

4th h. — ☋ 29:00 PBh

3rd h.

Valdivia Earthquake
Sun 05-22-1960
17:17:07
Valdivia, Maule
Chile
Timezone: 4 DST: 0
Latitude: 35S12'00
Longitude: 72W16'00
Ayanamsha : -23:18:10 Lahiri

9th h. — MC 11:50 Pus / ♅ 23:59 Asl

10th h. — ♀ 10:18 Mag / ☊ 29:00 UPh

2nd h.	1st h.	12th h.	11th h.
♄℞ 24:37 PSh / ♃℞ 08:42 Mul	ASC 00:24 Vis	♆℞ 13:49 Swa	

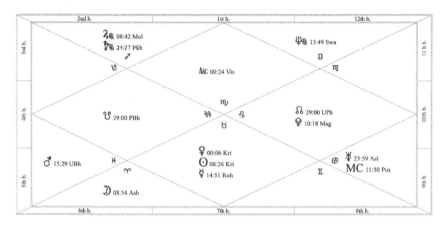

A modern mechanical cotton gin was created by American inventor Eli Whitney in 1793 and patented in 1794. Whitney's gin used a combination of a wire screen and small wire hooks to pull the cotton through, while brushes continuously removed the loose cotton lint to prevent jams. This was the beginning of the transformation for humanity using machines to do the work that was done manually before. This was the beginning of the industrial revolution.

In many inventions planet Uranus was with either Rahu or Ketu, the nodal axis. In this case Rahu was conjunct Uranus. Furthermore, Pluto was conjunct Ketu, meaning both Uranus and Pluto were opposed with Rahu and Ketu. This was an amazing time historically, changing the world forever. Pluto always indicates power, and this represented a new power for humanity. Rahu in Leo has always brought a new era with invention, leadership, and positive shifts within the world bringing new achievements and advancements.

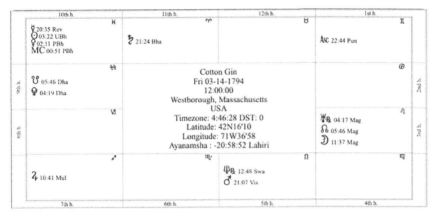

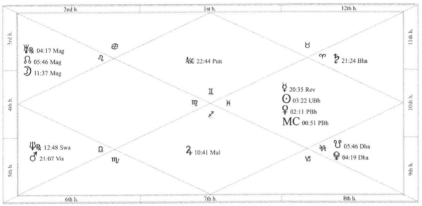

Rahu in Leo often coincides with the emergence of bold and visionary leaders who reshape political and societal landscapes. Some notable examples are listed below.

June 1904 – November 1905

- Theodore Roosevelt (USA): Won the 1904 USA. Presidential Election, securing his position as a strong leader of the Progressive Era.

July 1941 – February 1943

- Franklin D. Roosevelt (USA): Led the USA into World War II after the attack on Pearl Harbor (December 7, 1941), becoming a wartime leader of global significance.

- Winston Churchill (United Kingdom): Solidified his leadership during the darkest hours of WWII, especially after the Battle of Britain.

March 1960 – October 1961

• John F. Kennedy (USA): Elected as the 35th President of the USA in November 1960, inspiring a new generation with his vision and leadership.

October 1978 – May 1980

- Margaret Thatcher (United Kingdom): Elected as Prime Minister in 1979, becoming the first woman to hold the office in the UK, heralding a new era of conservatism.
- Ronald Reagan (USA): Declared his candidacy for the USA presidency in 1979, leading to his eventual election in 1980.

February 2016 – August 2017

- Donald Trump (USA): Elected as the 45th President of the USA in November 2016, marking a significant political shift.
- Emmanuel Macron (France): Elected as President of France in 2017, becoming one of the youngest leaders in French history.

Future Rahu in Leo August 2034 – February 2036

Based on historical trends, this period could bring the emergence of transformative leaders and major global changes.

Catastrophic Events Rahu in Leo and Ketu in Aquarius

- Great Kanto earthquake, this earthquake destroyed Tokyo and Yokohama September 1, 1923, killed 140,000 people.
- Great Chilean earthquake, VALDIVIA, May 22, 1960, killed 1,000 to 6,000 people.
- Mount St Helens eruption, volcanic eruption in Washington State, May 18, 1980, killed 57 people.
- 2nd Congo war, conflict in the Democratic Republic of Congo, August 2, 1998, killed 5.4 million people.
- Honduras hurricane Mitch, hurricane caused severe flooding in Central America, October 22, 1998, killed 1,100 people.
- Italian earthquake, earthquake in Italy central region, august 24, 2016 killed 299 people.

Predictions for August 12, 2034 to April 12, 2036 Rahu in Leo and Ketu in Aquarius

Predictions 2034

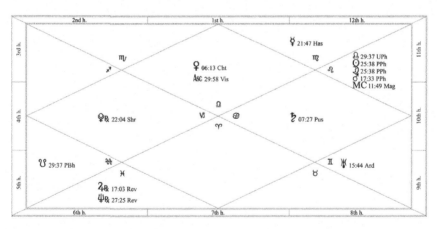

	6th h.	7th h.	8th h.	9th h.
	♓ ♆℞ 27:25 Rev ♃℞ 17:03 Rev	♈	♉	♊ ♅ 15:44 Ard
5th h.	♒ ☋ 29:37 PBh	September Solar Eclipse 34 Tue 09-12-2034 12:12:57 Washington, District of Columbia USA Timezone: 5 DST: 1 Latitude: 38N53'42 Longitude: 77W02'11 Ayanamsha : -24:20:29 Lahiri	♄ 07:27 Pus	♋ 10th h.
4th h.	♑ ♀℞ 22:04 Shr		MC 11:49 Mag ☉ 12:33 PPh ☿ 25:38 PPh ☊ 29:37 UPh	♌ 11th h.
	♐ 3rd h.	♏ ♀ 06:13 Cht ASC 29:58 Vis 2nd h.	♎ 1st h.	♍ ☿ 21:47 Has 12th h.

January 19, 2034, transiting Mars will conjunct Ketu, then soon after will conjunct Neptune on February 6, 2034. This represents illusions, a big fog whereas something is suppressed and not seen that involves a huge deception. This may involve storms that create a fog that is very disruptive to traveling by ship in the ocean. But more than likely it will indicate scandalous government coverups.

The most significant change in this year of 2034 is that transiting Saturn will go into Cancer, July 12, 2034. Cancer is the sign of security and protection and while Saturn is in this sign, people will tend to feel more insecure and feel the need for more protection. This will intensify as Saturn continues its transit through Cancer and opposes Pluto in approximately one year.

March 27, 2034, Jupiter will transit into Pisces and remain there until April 6, 2035. Jupiter is at home in the sign of Pisces and will inspire more spiritual thought and progressive thinking in psychology and philosophy. May 2, 2034, Jupiter will conjunct Ketu at 8° Pisces. This will inspire a deep quest for interest beyond this world, such as mysticism, spirituality, and exploration into the unknown. This could also increase interest in cults or other mind control manipulation. Be on the lookout for deceptive organizations that can manipulate people's minds. Throughout the year Jupiter is transiting close to Neptune, which will indicate great deception and illusions throughout this year. October 1, 2034, Mars will conjunct Rahu as they both come together at 29° of Leo. This fires up leadership throughout the world as there needs to be strength in power to give protection from dictators.

November 10, 2034, Mars will oppose Neptune at 25° Virgo/Pisces. Again, this is indicating extremes in deception and problems around manipulative mind controlling people and organizations. This is a year of scandals and corruption that surrounds governments globally.

The nodal axis in this position before produced intense and serious earthquakes. I predict this is the year that a big earthquake could hit California. Between August through September 2034 and specifically September 7, 2034, when Uranus will be at 15° Gemini and Mercury will be at 15° Virgo and Jupiter will be at 17° of Pisces, this forms a mutable T square that could activate earthquakes. The most destructive earthquake that hit San Francisco in 1906 involved this mutable axis with Neptune, Uranus, and Mercury at 15° in the mutable signs.

May 31, 2034, Mars will conjunct Uranus at 10° of Gemini causing upsets particularly in storms and severe weather globally. Within a week on June 6, 2034, Mars will then conjunct Saturn at 28° of Gemini and at the same time the Sun will conjunct Uranus at 12° of Gemini on the same day. This represents unexpected events concerning world leaders.

Particularly this will affect the leadership in the USA. There will be a sudden unexpected event with possible attacks and these surprises could create great loss.

Predictions 2035

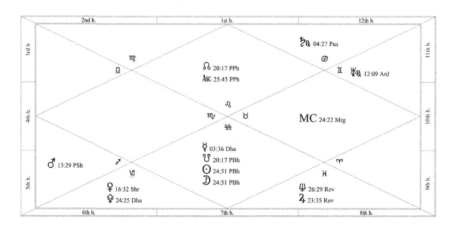

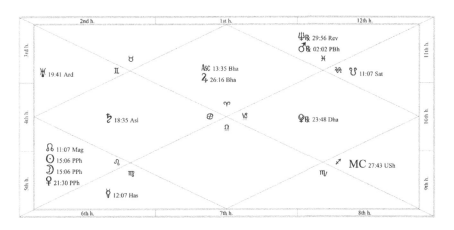

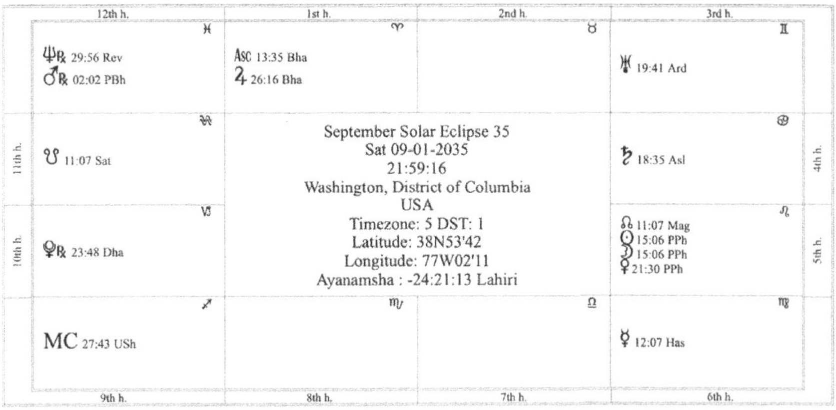

	12th h.		1st h.		2nd h.		3rd h.	
	♓		♈		♉		♊	
	♆℞ 29:56 Rev ♂℞ 02:02 PBh		ASC 13:35 Bha ♃ 26:16 Bha				♅ 19:41 Ard	

September Solar Eclipse 35
Sat 09-01-2035
21:59:16
Washington, District of Columbia
USA
Timezone: 5 DST: 1
Latitude: 38N53'42
Longitude: 77W02'11
Ayanamsha : -24:21:13 Lahiri

11th h. ☊ 11:07 Sat ♒ / ♄ 18:35 Asl ♋ 4th h.

10th h. ♀℞ 23:48 Dha ♑ / ☊ 11:07 Mag, ⊙ 15:06 PPh, ☽ 15:06 PPh, ♀ 21:30 PPh ♌ 5th h.

MC 27:43 USh ♐ / ♏ / ♎ / ☿ 12:07 Has ♍ 6th h.

9th h. | 8th h. | 7th h. | 6th h.

	2nd h.		1st h.		12th h.	

3rd h. / ♅ 19:41 Ard ♊ / ♉ / ASC 13:35 Bha ♃ 26:16 Bha / ♆℞ 29:56 Rev ♂℞ 02:02 PBh ♓ / ♒ ☊ 11:07 Sat 11th h.

4th h. / ♄ 18:35 Asl / ♈ / ♎ ♑ / ♀℞ 23:48 Dha 10th h.

5th h. / ☊ 11:07 Mag ⊙ 15:06 PPh ☽ 15:06 PPh ♀ 21:30 PPh ♌ ♍ / ☿ 12:07 Has / ♏ MC 27:43 USh 9th h.

6th h. | 7th h. | 8th h.

The most significant transit this year involves Neptune. It transits into Aries June 26, 2035, but will retrograde back into Pisces August 29, 2035, then again will transit forward into Aries April 15, 2036, and again go back into Pisces December 1, 2036. Then finally by February 5, 2036 Neptune will move into Aries where it will finally remain there for the next 12 years. So, the most important take away from all of this is that Neptune will be moving back and forth between the last degree of Pisces and the first degree of Aries, which is the last degree of a water sign and the first degree of a fire sign. This means Neptune throughout this duration will be gandanta. Gandanta is when planets are at the last degrees of a water sign and first degrees of a fire sign, and always means extreme turbulence. In this case it is in the last degree of the entire zodiac, which indicates incredible floods, storms, and major emotional turmoil throughout the world.

March 24 - 27, 2035 Jupiter will conjunct Neptune. On the positive side Neptune and Jupiter together at 26° - 27° of Pisces will activate a deep search for mysticism and spirituality. This can indicate revelations and revolutions or movements involving spiritual work. This could be a very productive year. There is great inspiration to transform oneself on a positive level. There will be a rise of motivational speakers that proclaim to revolutionize your life and elevate spiritual consciousness. But all at the same time, one will need to be weary of great deception, especially in cults that can control the mind in a negative way.

Jupiter will transit into Aries April 6, 2035 to April 14, 2036. Jupiter in Aries will give rise to a new motivation and inspiration to create new beginnings. Be open to new cutting-edge ideas and progress in the world of technology.

Jupiter will be gandanta at 29° Pisces March 30, 2035 to April 6, 2035. Be careful not to be swayed by your emotions and irrational unrealistic behavior and beliefs.

April 11, 2035, Mars will oppose Saturn indicating great stress but courage to overcome obstacles as Mars is exalted in Capricorn at this time giving it more power. Soon after May 14, 2035, Mars will conjunct Pluto at 25° of Capricorn, this indicates an overturn of power and resistance. On a positive note, this aspect can represent destruction but an overruling in government affairs.

Mars will be spending more time in the signs of Aquarius and Pisces as it will turn retrograde on August 15, 2035 at 4° Pisces and turn direct October 15, 2035, at 23° of Pisces. Because of the retrograde motion

Mars will be in Aquarius from May 22, 2035 to July 21, 2035, and during this time Mars will conjunct Ketu on June 15, 2035 at 14° of Aquarius. Mars and Ketu conjunctions are always dangerous. Be cautious and not overly impulsive or impatient around this time.

September 10, 2035 to November 17, 2035, Mars will be in Aquarius aligning with Ketu. Although they aren't exactly conjunct, this will give power away and struggles for world leaders. There is great turmoil and corruption prominent within the USA government during this time. The last time Ketu was in Aquarius and Rahu was in Leo was during the time that Trump was elected president the first time in 2016, and he was falsely accused for colluding with Russia. There will be many underhanded, and wrongful lies with undercurrents to demean and disrupt world leaders at this time.

October 17, 2035, Saturn, and Pluto are in opposition exactly at 23° Cancer and Capricorn indicating great power struggles. This can pertain to government corruption and even terrorist activity. It indicates a great fall in power is about to occur.

Predictions 2036

	6th h.	♓	7th h.	♈	8th h.	♉	9th h.	♊
	♀ 28:40 Rev ♇ 28:18 Rev		2 20:46 Bha ♂ 25:07 Bha				♅℞ 16:48 Ard	
5th h.	☉ 13:48 Sat ☽ 13:48 Sat ☊ 01:53 Dha	♒	February Solar Eclipse 36 Tue 02-26-2036 23:58:03 Washington, District of Columbia USA				♄℞ 19:43 Asl	10th h.
4th h.	☿ 27:15 Dha ♀ 25:33 Dha	♑	Timezone: 5 DST: 0 Latitude: 38N53'42 Longitude: 77W02'11 Ayanamsha : -24:21:35 Lahiri				☋ 01:53 Mag MC 07:45 Mag	11th h.
	3rd h.	♐	2nd h.	♏	Asc 26:54 Vis 1st h.	♎	12th h.	♍

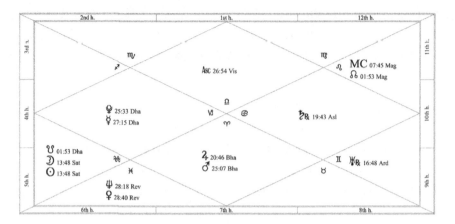

The first three months of the year Rahu is in Leo and Ketu in Aquarius and then they change signs April 12, 2036. During this time, the world is calm before the many changes and storms about to come.

Jupiter will conjunct Mars February 18, 2036 at 19° of Aries and around this time Saturn 20° Cancer is squaring this duo. There is a T square with Pluto 25° Capricorn opposing Saturn. This represents extreme power with controlling forces at odds with one another. This will involve major strife in governments around the world and extreme difficulties pertaining to money, wealth, power, and corruption within the government. Very powerful sources are attacking each other causing disruption and an unsettled feeling in the air. The ways that we exchange money and value in the world is going through a major transformation period.

CHAPTER 10

Rahu in Cancer and Ketu in Capricorn

April 12, 2036 to October 19, 2037

From all the events that took place during Rahu in Cancer and Ketu in Capricorn, it seems these placements create powerful and enormous storms indicating that this brings severity of weather with hurricanes, typhoons, and earthquakes.

There were also violent events involving mass shootings and a presidential assassination attempt. But one of the most promising events occurred with the signing of the Declaration of Independence, which gave the USA it's freedom from England. This can indicate this is a time to find freedom from injustice.

Nakshatras Activated

Rahu in Cancer (Punarvasu, Pushya, Ashlesha) and Ketu in Capricorn (Uttara Ashadha, Shravana, Dhanishta).

What happened before:

The placement of Rahu and Ketu in Cancer and Capricorn can affect the security of a nation. The most destructive earthquake to ever hit California destroyed the city of San Francisco in 1906, when Rahu was in Cancer and Ketu in Capricorn.

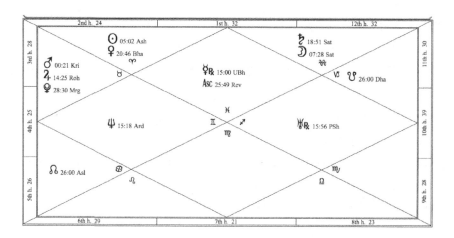

1st h. 32	2nd h. 24	3rd h. 28	4th h. 25
ASC 25:49 Rev ☿℞ 15:00 UBh	☉ 05:02 Ash ♀ 20:46 Bha	♂ 00:21 Kri ♃ 14:25 Roh ♀ 28:30 Mrg	♆ 15:18 Ard

12th h. 32 / 5th h. 26

| ♄ 18:51 Sat
☽ 07:28 Sat | San Francisco Earthquake
Wed 04-18-1906
05:12:00
San Francisco, California
USA
Timezone: 8 DST: 0
Latitude: 37N46'30
Longitude: 122W25'10
Ayanamsha : -22:32:42 Lahiri | ☊ 26:00 Asl |

11th h. 30 / 6th h. 29

| ☋ 26:00 Dha | | |

| ♅℞ 15:56 PSh | | |

| 10th h. 39 | 9th h. 28 | 8th h. 23 | 7th h. 21 |

2nd h. 24	1st h. 32	12th h. 32
☉ 05:02 Ash ♀ 20:46 Bha	☿℞ 15:00 UBh ASC 25:49 Rev	♄ 18:51 Sat ☽ 07:28 Sat

3rd h. 28 / 11th h. 30

| ♂ 00:21 Kri
♃ 14:25 Roh
♀ 28:30 Mrg | | ☋ 26:00 Dha |

4th h. 25 / 10th h. 39

| ♆ 15:18 Ard | | ♅℞ 15:56 PSh |

5th h. 26 / 9th h. 28

| ☊ 26:00 Asl | | |

| 6th h. 29 | 7th h. 21 | 8th h. 23 |

The 2017 Las Vegas shooting was a tragic mass shooting that occurred on October 1, 2017, during the Route 91 Harvest Music Festival. A lone gunman opened fire on the crowd from his hotel room, killing 58 people and injuring or wounding over 850 others as they fled the gunfire. The shooting was the deadliest mass shooting in modern USA history and had a profound impact on the nation, prompting discussions on gun control, security measures at public events, and the need for mental health support for survivors and first responders.

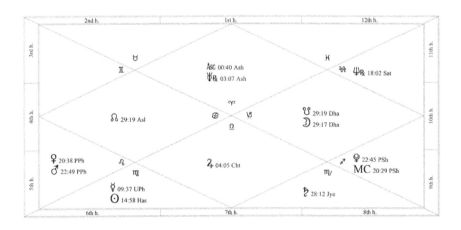

Bubonic Plague 1665-1667

This was the worst outbreak of a plague in England since the black death of 1348. London lost roughly 15% of its population. While 68,596 deaths were recorded in the city, the true number was probably over 100,000 people. Other parts of the country also suffered.

The earliest cases of disease occurred in the spring of 1665 in a parish outside the city walls called St Giles-in-the-Fields. The death rate began to rise during the hot summer months and peaked in September 1666 when 7,165 Londoners died in one week.

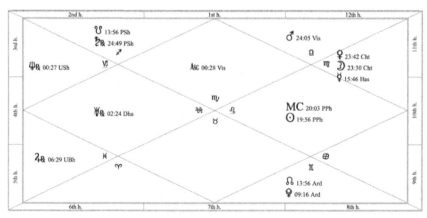

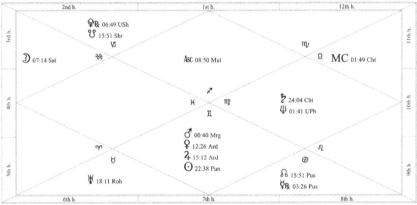

This is the chart I use for the birth of the USA as it is the chart for the signing of the Declaration of Independence.

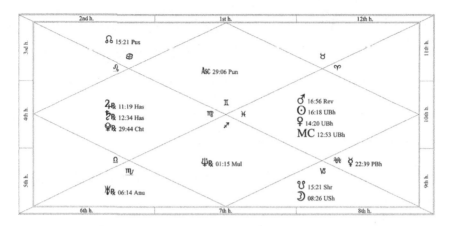

On March 30, 1981, Ronald Reagan, the president of the USA was shot and wounded by John Hinckley Jr. in Washington, D.C., as Reagan was returning to his limousine after a speaking engagement.

Reagan was seriously wounded by a revolver bullet that ricocheted off the side of the presidential limousine and hit him in the left underarm, breaking a rib, puncturing a lung, and causing serious internal bleeding. He was close to death upon arrival at George Washington University Hospital, but was stabilized in the emergency room; he then underwent emergency exploratory surgery. He recovered and was released from the hospital on April 11, 1981.

Catastrophic Events with Rahu in Cancer and Ketu in Capricorn

- San Francisco earthquake, earthquake and fire that devastated San Francisco April 18, 1906, killed 3,000 people.
- Iraq Iran war, prolonged war between Iran and Iraq, September 22, 1980, killed 500,000 -1,000,000 people.
- Odisha, India cyclone, cyclone impacted Odisha, October 29, 1999, killed 9,658 people.
- Puerto Rico hurricane Maria devastating hurricane in Puerto Rico, September 20, 2017, killed 2,975 people.
- Hurricane Harvey, impacted Texas, August 25, 2017, killed 107 people.
- Hurricane Irma, hurricane affected Caribbean and Florida, September 10, 2017, killed 134 people.
- California campfire, devastating wildfire in northern California, November 8, 2018 killed 85 people.
- Hurricane Michael, category 5 hurricane struck Florida, October 10, 2018, killed 74 people.

Predictions for April 12, 2036 to October 19, 2027 – Rahu in Cancer and Ketu in Capricorn

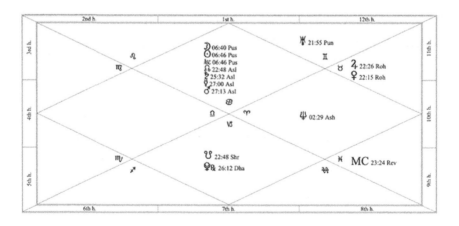

The July solar eclipse chart is an extraordinary display of extremes where planets are grouped in a Stellium indicating intense events involving massive breakouts of power and possible war. The most striking aspect in this chart is Rahu conjunct Saturn and Mars opposed Pluto with Ketu. The most interesting thing concerning this chart is that in the birth chart for the USA, all these planets in Cancer, Mars, Mercury, Saturn, Rahu, Sun, and Moon, fall in the 8th house of the USA chart. The 8th house represents huge corporate money, corruption, secrets, scandals, and even death.

There will be massive events surrounding control, power, and money this year. The fact that Pluto and Saturn are tied up with the Rahu and Ketu axis indicate this will be one of the most extreme years with the government of the USA. There will be an overturn of power and revelations with corruption mixed in with the extremes of scandalous affairs.

There is a breakdown within the government of the USA vastly affecting the freedoms that the USA was founded on. This looks like there could be another revolution.

August 27, 2036, Saturn will go into Leo where it will remain for the next two years. Saturn does not operate well in this sign; therefore, the economy is struggling, and Jupiter is in Taurus, which is not very good for Jupiter. They are forming a square. During this time, the economy is working hard to make a comeback and is in a period of growth, but valiant efforts will help many industries change for the better.

Predictions 2037

5th h.			6th h.	7th h.		8th h.	
		♓	♈		♉		♊
♆ 29:44 Rev			♃℞ 22:45 Roh		♅℞ 22:49 Pun		
		♒	Janurary Solar Eclipse 37				⊕
			Fri 01-16-2037		☋ 13:36 Pus		
			04:34:30				
			Washington, District of Columbia				
		♑	USA				♌
♀ 25:47 Dha			Timezone: 5 DST: 0		♄℞ 07:28 Mag		
☌ 13:36 Shr			Latitude: 38N53'42				
☽ 02:13 USh			Longitude: 77W02'11				
☉ 02:13 USh			Ayanamsha : -24:22:16 Lahiri				
		♐	♏		♎		♍
♀ 16:40 PSh			ASC 20:08 Jye			MC 08:37 UPh	
☿ 08:36 Mul			♂ 24:13 Jye				
2nd h.			1st h.	12th h.		11th h.	

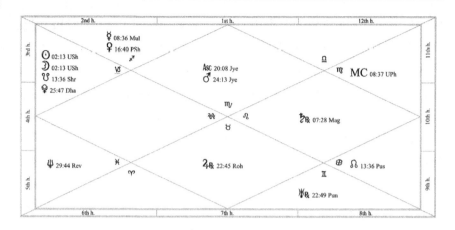

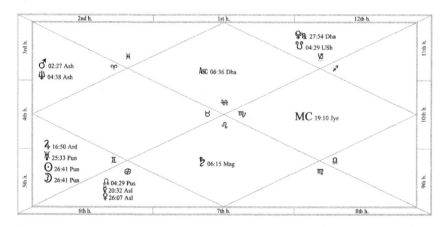

March 22, 2037, Mars will conjunct Ketu at 11° of Capricorn where Mars is extraordinarily strong in its exaltation sign. This empowers invention and technology, especially concerning vehicles and cars. Mars and Ketu conjunctions can pertain to hostility, anger, and attacks, this is the combination of terrorism.

July 16, 2037, Mars will conjunct Neptune at 4° Aries indicating great deception where something is brewing under the surface that cannot be seen. There are hostile events about to occur and this is where it all begins.

Jupiter will be in Gemini April 26, 2037 to September 16, 2037. Jupiter will go into Cancer September 16, 2037 to January 17, 2038. Then again Jupiter will return to Gemini January 17, 2038 to May 11, 2038. During the time that Jupiter is in Gemini it will open new levels of communication and travel with amazing inventions never seen throughout humanity's evolution. September 9, 2037, Jupiter will conjunct Uranus at 28° Gemini, which indicates incredible new inventions in technology. There are so many indications of technological advancement and progress throughout this year. September 16, 2037, Jupiter will transit into Cancer aligning with Rahu, and on September 27, 2037, Jupiter will conjunct Rahu at 1° of Cancer. As Jupiter aligns with Rahu, we can expect major and colossal events that change the world forever. This indicates an awakening!

October 12, 2037, Mars will turn retrograde at 11° to12° of Taurus. Mars will remain retrograde until December 23, 2037, where it will turn direct at 25° Aries. While Mars is in Taurus from August 29, 2037 to November 27, 2037, it will be forming a square to Saturn. This will cause great difficulty within the economy because Taurus rules finances and money.

Mars will be in Aries from November 27, 2037 to January 18, 2038, which makes Mars more powerful and intense being in its own sign. This can activate forward growth and progress in industry, but also trigger anger, hostility, and warlike behavior.

October 19, 2037, Rahu enters Gemini and Ketu enters Sagittarius. This is an enormous turning point as Rahu and Ketu are most volatile in these signs. October 20, 2037, Uranus will exactly conjunct Rahu at 29° of Gemini instigating incredible change, and sudden unexpected explosive events. We are on the verge of another catastrophic event in humanity.

CHAPTER 11

Rahu in Gemini and Ketu in Sagittarius

October 19, 2037 to April 07, 2039

Rahu in Gemini and Ketu in Sagittarius are the most difficult signs for the nodes to be in, and these placements are what prompted me to write this book. As you know, every 18 1/2-year cycle when they are in these signs there was always a catastrophic event. This theory will be proven by looking back at all the events that took place while Rahu was in Gemini and Ketu in Sagittarius. Some of these events were more severe than others based on the other planets involved. We will be able to decipher what is ahead for the next 18 months based on past events concerning these placements.

Nakshatras Activated

Rahu in Gemini (Mrigashira, Ardra, Punarvasu) and Ketu in Sagittarius (Mula, Purva Ashadha, Uttara Ashadha).

What happened before:

As you can see there were many more events during this time indicating just how extreme these placements are.

Here is the list in sequential order going back 18 ½ years each time Rahu was in Gemini and Ketu in Sagittarius:

- 2020 – Covid19,
- 2001 – September 11, 2001 terror attack on USA
- 1982 – AIDS virus
- 1969 – Kennedy Assassination
- 1945 – Bombing of Hiroshima, Japan

This is the most treacherous portion of the zodiac for Rahu and Ketu. While Rahu was in Gemini in the nakshatra Ardra, the most horrific events occurred – the bombing of Hiroshima in 1945, assassination of President John F. Kennedy in 1963, and the 9/11 attacks on America in 2001. For all these dates, Rahu was in Gemini in the nakshatra Ardra. Saturn was conjunct Rahu for the Hiroshima bomb. On 9/11 Jupiter was conjunct Rahu, and Mars was conjunct Ketu.

These horrific events are associated with the birth chart of the USA, where four powerful planets (Mars, Venus, Sun, and Jupiter) occupy the sign of Gemini. Obviously, there appears to be a connection between events and the charts of the countries where these events are likely to occur.

Ardra is ruled by the storm god Rudra symbolized by the howling wind and the tear drop. It is the nakshatra of tragic events. Gemini as an air sign indicates messages or tragedy through the air or transportation. Bombs were dropped by aircraft on Hiroshima. Airplanes were used as weapons of mass destruction in 9/11 in New York. President Kennedy was traveling in a vehicle when he was shot.

Ketu in Sagittarius is a difficult place, particularly in the nakshatra Mula. This nakshatra indicates destruction because Niritti, the goddess of destruction rules over Mula. Furthermore, this is the point of the Galactic Center where astronomers have detected the largest concentration of black holes in the Universe. Black holes are known to be like a vacuum and could be the entry to other dimensions.

The area following Mula in Sagittarius is Purva Ashadha which is known for declarations of war. Many times, the nodes passing through this portion of the zodiac can bring war.

As horrific as these events have been in history, the signs and nakshatras are part of an evolution that eventually brings opportunities for healing. Destruction clears the path for rebuilding. The nakshatra following Ardra is Punarvasu, which means the return of the light. Even after the darkest storms comes a sunny day.

As the nodes transit through Gemini and Sagittarius, the truth that is revealed comes through our worst nightmares, violence, death, and sorrow. It is the release of the buildup from mounting pressure. Just as deep emotion produces tears, so too do storm clouds as they accumulate moisture, and then burst with rain. What comes out of the dark, or is revealed at that time, are issues surrounding suffering and pain. What comes out of tragedy is the unity of people to heal the suffering and pain of isolation.

The fixed star Betelgeuse around 4°-5° of Gemini is known to produce assassinations, explosions, and lightning.

The Great Chicago Fire burned from Sunday to early Tuesday, October 8-10, 1871. The fire killed approximately 300 people, destroyed roughly 3.3 square miles of Chicago, and left more than 100,000 residents homeless. Saturn was conjunct Ketu in Mula.

The AIDS epidemic killed more people than any disease over time. The first AIDS case recognized in the USA was in 1982, with Rahu in Gemini, Ketu in Sagittarius.

Chart 1 — Hiroshima Attack (South Indian style)

	♂ 16:10 Roh ♅ 23:23 Mrg	♀ 08:42 Ard ☊ 15:48 Ard ♄ 25:07 Pun ☽ 26:12 Pun
7th h. 25	8th h. 37	9th h. 25	10th h. 31

| 6th h. 32 | Hiroshima Attack | ♆ 16:52 Asl ☉ 20:07 Asl | 11th h. 31 |

| 5th h. 28 | Mon 08-06-1945 10:35:23 Hiroshima Japan Timezone: -9 DST: 0 Latitude: 34N23'00 Longitude: 132E28'00 Ayanamsha : -23:05:34 Lahiri | ☿ 11:41 Mag | 12th h. 27 |

| 4th h. 27 | ☋ 15:48 PSh | 3rd h. 26 | 2nd h. 25 | ♃ 03:12 UPh ♇ 11:15 Has ASC 24:08 Cht | 1st h. 23 |

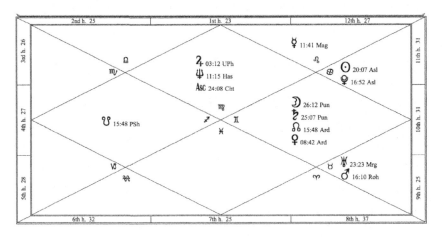

Chart 2 — North Indian style

☿ 11:41 Mag

♃ 03:12 UPh ♇ 11:15 Has ASC 24:08 Cht

☉ 20:07 Asl ♆ 16:52 Asl

☋ 15:48 PSh

☽ 26:12 Pun ♄ 25:07 Pun ☊ 15:48 Ard ♀ 08:42 Ard

♅ 23:23 Mrg ♂ 16:10 Roh

2nd h. 25 · 1st h. 23 · 12th h. 27 · 11th h. 31 · 3rd h. 26 · 4th h. 27 · 5th h. 28 · 6th h. 32 · 7th h. 25 · 8th h. 37 · 9th h. 25 · 10th h. 31

Chart 3 — John F Kennedy Assassinated (South Indian style)

♃℞ 16:28 UBh			☊ 18:34 Ard
3rd h. 31	4th h. 28	5th h. 20	6th h. 30

| 2nd h. 24 | John F Kennedy Assassinated | | 7th h. 25 |

| ♄ 23:57 Dha ☽ 17:37 Shr ASC 16:28 Shr | Fri 11-22-1963 12:00:00 Dallas, Texas USA Timezone: 6 DST: 0 Latitude: 32N46'59 Longitude: 96W48'24 Ayanamsha : -23:20:52 Lahiri | ♅ 16:27 PPh ♀ 20:43 PPh | 8th h. 31 |
| 1st h. 31 | | | |

| ☋ 18:34 PSh | ☉ 06:21 Anu ☿ 16:22 Anu ♂ 27:09 Jye ♇ 28:04 Jye | ♆ 22:34 Vis | |
| 12th h. 19 | 11th h. 34 | 10th h. 27 | 9th h. 37 |

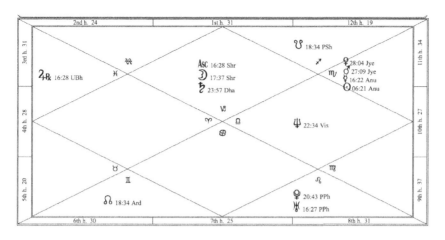

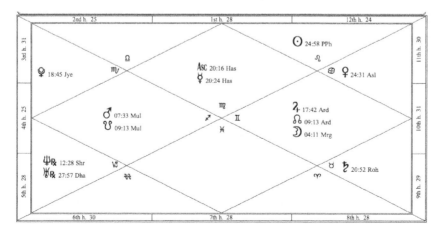

Top chart (AIDS)

11th h.	12th h.	1st h.	2nd h.
♓	♈	ASC 26:36 Mrg · ♉	☊ 28:21 Pun · ♊

10th h.			3rd h.
☉ 09:08 Sat / MC 03:25 Dha · ♒	AIDS Sun 02-21-1982 12:00:00 Washington, District of Columbia USA Timezone: 5 DST: 0 Latitude: 38N53'42 Longitude: 77W02'11 Ayanamsha : -23:36:12 Lahiri		♋

9th h.			4th h.
☽ 13:30 Shr / ☿ 12:49 Shr / ♀ 01:58 USh · ♑			♌

8th h.	7th h.	6th h.	5th h.
☋ 28:21 USh · ♇ 03:04 Mul · ♐	♅ 10:54 Anu · ♏	♀R 03:10 Cht · ♃ 16:42 Swa · ♎	♂R 25:34 Cht · ♄R 28:14 Cht · ♍

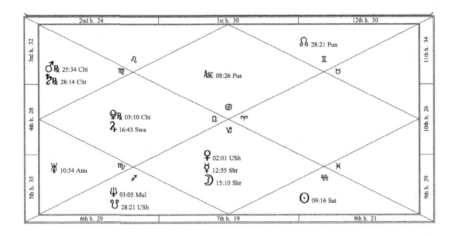

Middle chart (North Indian)

2nd h. 24 — 1st h. 30 — 12th h. 30 — 11th h. 34 — 10th h. 26 — 9th h. 29 — 8th h. 21 — 7th h. 19 — 6th h. 29 — 5th h. 35 — 4th h. 28 — 3rd h. 32

- ☊ 28:21 Pun
- ♂R 25:34 Cht · ♄R 28:14 Cht
- ASC 08:26 Pus
- ♀R 03:10 Cht · ♃ 16:43 Swa
- ♅ 10:54 Anu
- ♇ 03:05 Mul · ☋ 28:21 USh
- ♀ 02:01 USh · ☿ 12:55 Shr · ☽ 15:10 Shr
- ☉ 09:16 Sat

Bottom chart (Chicago Fire)

4th h. 23	5th h. 26	6th h. 39	7th h. 26
♓	♇R 00:48 Ash · ♀R 27:25 Kri · ♈	♉	☊ 02:31 Mrg · ♊

3rd h. 32			8th h. 34
♒	Chicago Fire Sun 10-08-1871 12:00:00 Chicago, Illinois USA Timezone: 5:50:35 DST: 0 Latitude: 41N51'00 Longitude: 87W39'00 Ayanamsha : -22:03:41 Lahiri		♃ 05:27 Pus · ♅ 08:46 Pus · ☽ 15:10 Pus · ♋

2nd h. 24			9th h. 24
♑			♌

1st h. 30	12th h. 22	11th h. 26	10th h. 31
♄ 11:59 Mul · ASC 02:35 Mul · ☋ 02:31 Mul · ♐	♂ 16:03 Anu · ♍	♎	♀R 04:22 UPh · ☿ 06:31 UPh · ☉ 22:56 Has · ♍

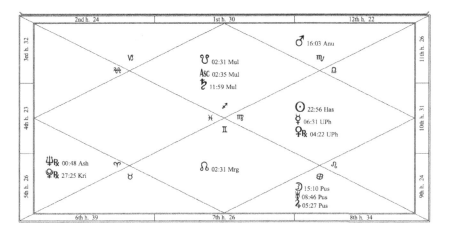

Peshtigo Fire October 8, 1871

This fire dates back to October 8, 1871. A fire that most likely would've been controllable and manageable evolved into a fire that spread over 1,875 square miles due to fierce winds and killed approximately 1,500 people. While it happened nearly 150 years ago, the Peshtigo Fire is still considered one of the worst disasters in USA history.

1st h.		2nd h.		3rd h.		4th h.	
	♓	☊℞ 00:48 Ash ♀℞ 27:25 Kri	♈		♉		♊
ASC 13:07 UBh		Peshtigo Fire Sun 10-08-1871 17:02:17 Peshtigo, Wisconsin USA Timezone: 5:51:00 DST: 0 Latitude: 45N03'16 Longitude: 87W44'57 Ayanamsha : -22:03:41 Lahiri		☋ 02:30 Mrg			
12th h.	♒			♃ 05:29 Pus ♅ 08:46 Pus ☽ 17:45 Asl	♋		5th h.
11th h.	♑				♌		6th h.
♄ 12:00 Mul MC 10:24 Mul ☊ 02:30 Mul	♐	♂ 16:12 Anu	♏		♎	♀℞ 04:18 UPh ☿ 06:49 UPh ☉ 23:08 Has	♍
10th h.		9th h.		8th h.		7th h.	

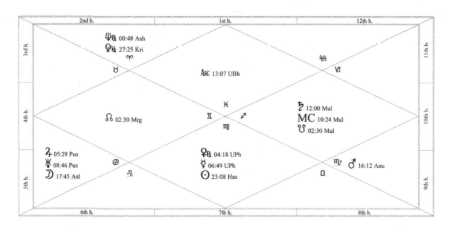

Bubonic Plague 1665-1667

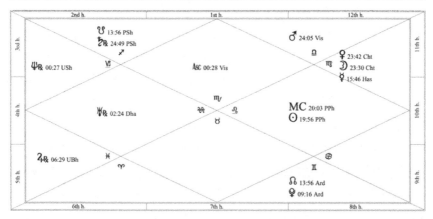

This was the worst outbreak of plague in England since the black death of 1348. London lost roughly 15% of its population. While 68,596 deaths were recorded in the city, the true number was probably over 100,000 people. Other parts of the country also suffered.

The earliest cases of disease occurred in the spring of 1665 in a parish outside the city walls called St Giles-in-the-Fields. The death rate began to rise during the hot summer months and peaked in September 1666 when 7,165 Londoners died in one week.

Catastrophic Events Rahu in Gemini and Ketu in Sagittarius

- Great fire of London, fire destroyed much of London, September 2, 1666.
- Peshtigo fire, deadliest fire in USA history in Wisconsin, October 8, 1871, killed more than1,500 people.
- Messina earthquake and tsunami destroyed Messina, Italy, December 28, 1908, killed 75,000 -100,000 people.
- Chinese civil war between nationalist and communist, August 1, 1927, killed 2.5 million people.
- Gujarat earthquake, Gujarat, India January 26, 2001, killed 20,000 people.
- El Salvador earthquake, struck El Salvador, January 13, 2001, killed 944 people.
- 9/11 attacks, terrorist attacks in USA, September 11, 2001, killed 2,977 people.
- Cyclone Idai, affected Mozambique, March 14, 2019, killed 1,303 people.
- Beirut port explosion, massive explosion in Beirut, August 4, 2020, killed 218 people.

Here is what I wrote about 2019 -2020 in my Book Rahu and Ketu our Karmic Destiny - written in 2017 based on the theory that Rahu in Gemini and Ketu in Sagittarius bring devasting and catastrophic events. I predicted with the chart (Major Event) that there would be a catastrophic event that would change history as we know it. Covid absolutely did!

Future Predictions – Rahu and Ketu our Karmic Destiny (written in 2017)

"Based on the analysis of history, the years of 2019-2020 looked like a dangerous time. Rahu will be in Gemini, Ketu in Sagittarius. In May 2019, Rahu will be with Mars, and Ketu with Saturn.

By the end of 2019 Saturn and Jupiter will conjoin Ketu in Mula while Rahu occupies the nakshatra Ardra. In January 2020 Saturn will conjoin Pluto and Jupiter while Ketu is in Mula, and Rahu is in Ardra. This will produce an event that will shake the world. By the end of January 2020, Saturn will transit into Capricorn while Mars is in Scorpio. They will thus flank Jupiter and Ketu (in Sagittarius), placing them in a combination known as papa kartari, flanked on either side by malefics.

Jupiter and Ketu in nakshatras Purva Ashadha and Uttara Ashadha may herald war because this is the nakshatra for the beginning of war.

From February 8, 2020 to March 23, 2020, Mars will be in Sagittarius with Jupiter. On February 25, 2020 Mars will conjoin Ketu in Mula while Rahu is in Ardra. This could be a time for catastrophic events since Jupiter magnifies the circumstances. During this time, transiting Saturn and Pluto will be together in Capricorn. This suggests the breakdown of corruption in governments.

There's a solar eclipse on December 26, 2019, at 10° Sagittarius. Transiting Mars will cross this degree on February 21-23, 2020. Mars will be in Mula, just two 2° from Ketu and in the same sign with Jupiter, while Rahu is in Ardra. This is very similar to the aspects that were operating at the time of 9/11. The difference is that Jupiter was conjunct Rahu, but this time is with Ketu."

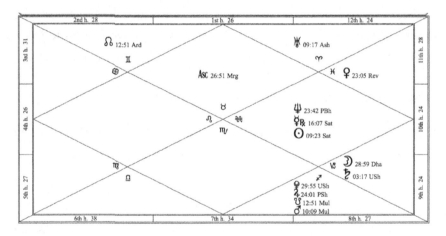

11th h. 28	12th h. 24	1st h. 26	2nd h. 28
♀ 23:05 Rev	♅ 09:17 Ash	ASC 26:51 Mrg	☊ 12:51 Ard
10th h. 24 — ♆ 23:42 PBh, ☿℞ 16:07 Sat, ☉ 09:23 Sat	Major Event Sat 02-22-2020 12:00:00 Washington, District of Columbia USA Timezone: 5 DST: 0 Latitude: 38N53'42 Longitude: 77W02'11 Ayanamsha : -24:08:03 Lahiri		3rd h. 31
9th h. 24 — ☽ 28:59 Dha, ♄ 03:17 USh			4th h. 26
♀ 29:55 USh, ♃ 24:01 PSh, ☋ 12:51 Mul, ♂ 10:09 Mul			
8th h. 27	7th h. 34	6th h. 38	5th h. 27

Therefore, from this observation I am making another powerful prediction for the time Rahu goes into Gemini and Ketu into Sagittarius 2037 -2038.

Predictions for October 19, 2037 to April 07, 2039 - Rahu in Gemini and Ketu in Sagittarius

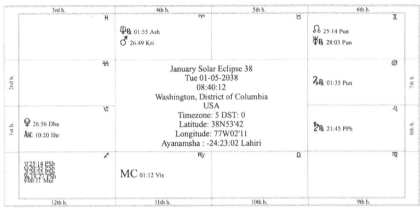

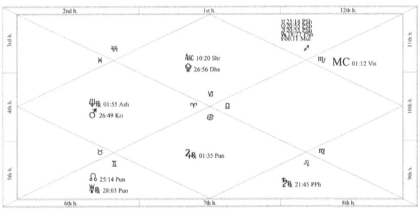

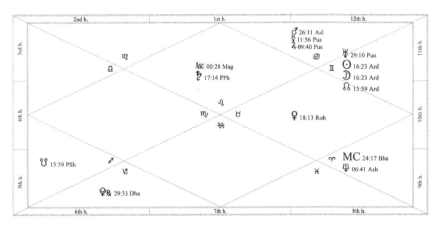

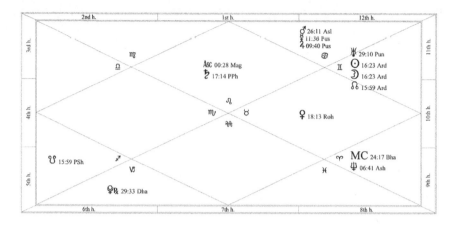

During the time that Rahu is in Gemini and Ketu is in Sagittarius and the eclipses are falling in these signs, many events are being activated. Powerful planets are converging together with the nodal axis and Mars is a major trigger that will be aspecting these planets from April through May of 2038.

Uranus will conjunct Jupiter March 21, 2038, at 25° Gemini, this will activate major advancements in travel and communications. There will be significant technological advances that are beyond what we could have imagined.

Mars will exactly conjunct Rahu April 29, 2038, which indicates extremes in violence and anger along with possible attacks and or pandemics. As Mars continues to transit through the sign of Gemini it will then conjunct Uranus May 14, 2038 at 26° Gemini. Mars will then transit out of Gemini into Cancer and conjunct Jupiter May 22, 2038 at 1° of Cancer. Therefore, Mars is the triggering action as it crosses over Rahu, Uranus, and Jupiter. So much will be occurring, one enormous event after another during this time.

Jupiter will transit into Cancer May 11, 2038, and remain there until March 3, 2039. Then July 16, 2038 Uranus will transit into the sign of Cancer, where it will remain for the next seven years. While both Jupiter and Uranus are transiting into Cancer there will be an incredible healing from the recent events that occurred. Jupiter is the planet of spirituality, philosophy, and expansion. While Jupiter is transiting through its most powerful sign of exaltation it will create a revival and a much-needed healing. This transit could also indicate a spiritual awakening for many on the planet.

Based on the previous events, I believe the most volatile time is between April and May of 2038. My assessment is based on the time when Mars, Uranus, and Jupiter all align in the sign of Gemini. This combination is extremely dangerous, indicating unexpected sudden and warlike events. The date I have chosen here is significant because Mars is at 20° of Gemini which is opposing the previous eclipse degree from the January 5, 2038, solar eclipse. On September 11, 2001, Mars opposed the previous eclipse degree exactly on that day. Therefore, based on previous events May 3, 2038, is a powerful day for radical events. With this knowledge it is time to take caution, and protection therefore it is not a day to be traveling or in crowded places. Regardless, if this is the exact day of an event the time between April and May must be taken with great caution.

9th h.		10th h.	11th h.		12th h.	
	♓	MC 02:09 Ash	♈	♉	☋ 17:40 Ard	♊
☿ 23:33 Rev		♇ 04:57 Ash			♂ 20:34 Pun	
♀ 07:39 UBh		☽ 11:02 Ash			⛢ 26:16 Pun	
		☉ 18:56 Bha			♃ 28:52 Pun	
	♒	Explosive Day!				♋
8th h.		Mon 05-03-2038			ASC 13:19 Pus	1st h.
		12:00:00				
		Washington, District of Columbia				
	♑	USA				♌
7th h.		Timezone: 5 DST: 1			♄℞ 15:02 PPh	3rd h.
♀ 29:45 Dha		Latitude: 38N53'42				
		Longitude: 77W02'11				
		Ayanamsha : -24:23:15 Lahiri				
	♐		♏	♎		♍
☊ 17:40 PSh						
6th h.		5th h.	4th h.		3rd h.	

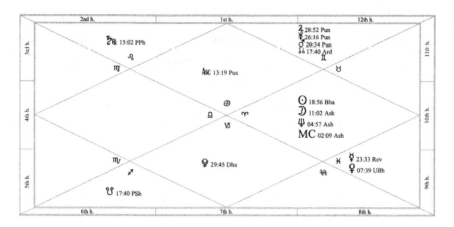

CHAPTER 12

Rahu in Taurus and Ketu in Scorpio

April 07, 2039 to December 09, 2040

Since Rahu and Ketu are said to be exalted in these positions, this means they are in their most powerful positions to manifest discoveries and positive events in the world. There seems to be the least number of tragedies during this time. Since it follows the period right after the most tragic events this indicates the nodal axis in Taurus and Scorpio bring about a profound healing. It is interesting that the discovery of penicillin that saves so many lives came about during Rahu in Taurus and in Ketu in Scorpio.

Therefore, this time in 2039 should be about healing from the drastic effects of Rahu in Gemini and Ketu in Sagittarius that just occurred 2037 through 2038.

Nakshatras Activated

Rahu in Taurus (Krittika, Rohini, Mrigashira) and Ketu in Scorpio (Vishaka, Anuradha, Jyeshta).

What happened before:

In the fixed signs of Taurus and Scorpio, things seem to consolidate and deepen. This may be the time that discoveries and revelations surface.

On a positive note, Alexander Fleming discovered penicillin in 1928 while Ketu was in Scorpio (with Saturn). This saved many lives and was a huge medical breakthrough for the world. It seems the nodes in Taurus/Scorpio give good results. This could be due to the exaltation of the nodes in these signs. Rahu is exalted in Taurus and Ketu exalted in Scorpio.

This is the time that Japan reorganized their country after World War II and made a remarkable industrial comeback after such widespread destruction.

It seems this portion of the zodiac facilitates the revelation of discoveries to make the world a better place. Remember, healings result after deep turmoil and devastation.

5th h. 32	6th h. 29	7th h. 20	8th h. 27
♅℞ 12:33 UBh ☽ 01:28 PBh	♃℞ 16:09 Bha	☊ 09:11 Kri	♂ 05:14 Mrg ♀ 25:26 Pun
4th h. 34	Penicillin Fri 09-28-1928 12:00:00 Washington, District of Columbia USA		**9th h. 30**
3rd h. 31	Timezone: 5 DST: 0 Latitude: 38N53'42 Longitude: 77W02'11 Ayanamsha : -22:51:27 Lahiri	♆ 07:22 Mag	**10th h. 36**
☋ 09:11 Anu ♄ 21:04 Jye ASC 23:41 Jye	♀ 06:24 Cht ☿ 08:08 Swa	☉ 12:27 Has	
2nd h. 25	1st h. 24	12th h. 17	11th h. 32

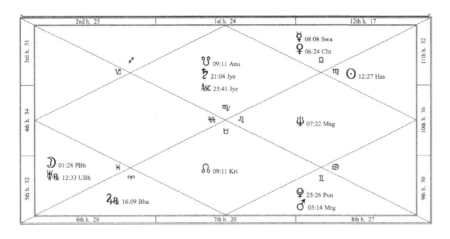

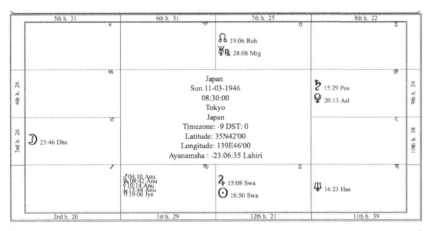

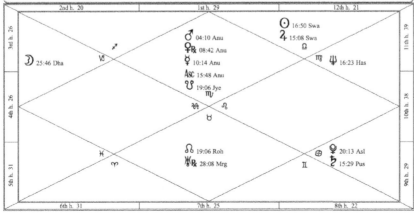

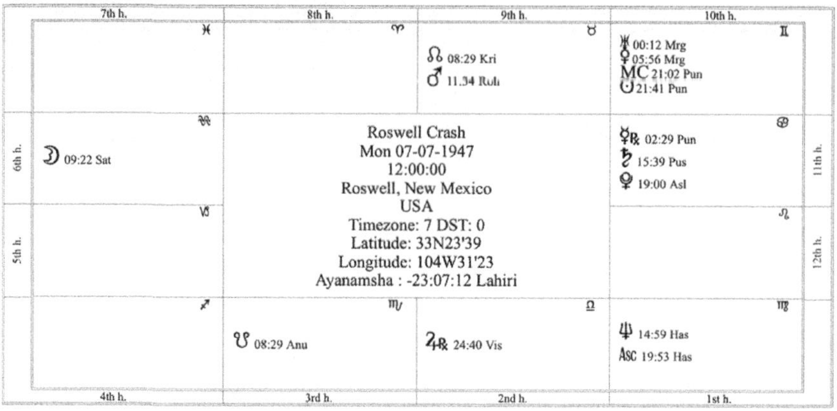
7th h.
8th h.
9th h.
10th h.
♓
♈
♉ ☊ 08:29 Kri
♂ 11.34 Roh
♊ ♅ 00:12 Mrg
♀ 05:56 Mrg
MC 21:02 Pun
☉ 21:41 Pun
6th h.
♒ ☽ 09:22 Sat
Roswell Crash
Mon 07-07-1947
12:00:00
Roswell, New Mexico
USA
Timezone: 7 DST: 0
Latitude: 33N23'39
Longitude: 104W31'23
Ayanamsha : -23:07:12 Lahiri
11th h.
♋ ☿℞ 02:29 Pun
♄ 15:39 Pus
♇ 19:00 Asl
5th h.
♑
12th h.
♌
♐
♏ ☋ 08:29 Anu
♎ ♃℞ 24:40 Vis
♍ ♆ 14:59 Has
Asc 19:53 Has
4th h.
3rd h.
2nd h.
1st h.

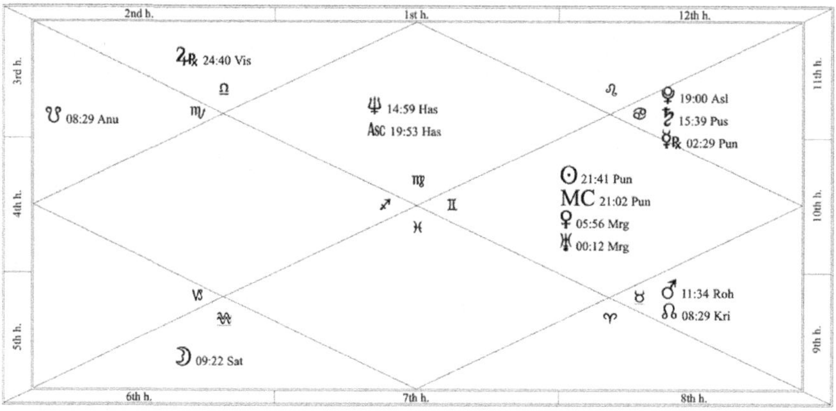
2nd h.
1st h.
12th h.
3rd h.
♃℞ 24:40 Vis
♎
♏
☋ 08:29 Anu
♆ 14:59 Has
Asc 19:53 Has
♌
♋
♇ 19:00 Asl
♄ 15:39 Pus
☿℞ 02:29 Pun
11th h.
4th h.
♍
♐
♊
♓
☉ 21:41 Pun
MC 21:02 Pun
♀ 05:56 Mrg
♅ 00:12 Mrg
10th h.
♑
♒
☽ 09:22 Sat
♉
♈
♂ 11:34 Roh
☊ 08:29 Kri
5th h.
9th h.
6th h.
7th h.
8th h.

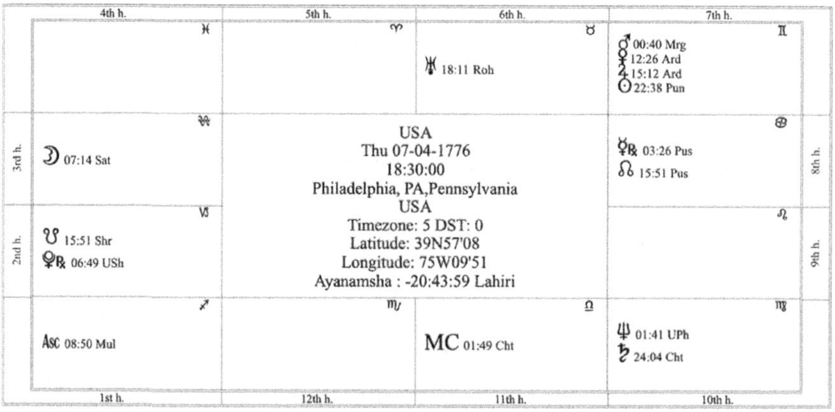
4th h.
5th h.
6th h.
7th h.
♓
♈
♉ ♅ 18:11 Roh
♊ ♂ 00:40 Mrg
♀ 12:26 Ard
♃ 15:12 Ard
☉ 22:38 Pun
3rd h.
♒ ☽ 07:14 Sat
USA
Thu 07-04-1776
18:30:00
Philadelphia, PA,Pennsylvania
USA
Timezone: 5 DST: 0
Latitude: 39N57'08
Longitude: 75W09'51
Ayanamsha : -20:43:59 Lahiri
8th h.
♋ ☿℞ 03:26 Pus
☊ 15:51 Pus
2nd h.
♑ ☋ 15:51 Shr
♇℞ 06:49 USh
9th h.
♌
♐ Asc 08:50 Mul
♏
♎ MC 01:49 Cht
♍ ♆ 01:41 UPh
♄ 24:04 Cht
1st h.
12th h.
11th h.
10th h.

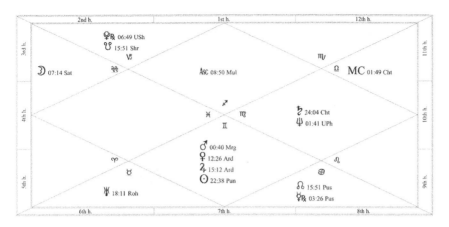

The Roswell incident is a conspiracy theory which alleges that the 1947 USA Army Air Forces balloon debris that was recovered near Roswell, New Mexico was actually a crashed extraterrestrial spacecraft. Many UFO proponents claim that the Roswell debris was in fact derived from an alien craft and accused the USA government of a cover-up.

It is fascinating to note the connections with this crash chart and the USA chart. The Sun and Moon are almost the same degrees and Uranus in the crash chart aligns with Mars in the USA chart. This Mars and Uranus alignment can mean we may have received new ideas for our own technology from this crash. Mars represents mechanics and Uranus rules technology. Furthermore, Saturn from the crash chart sits on the USA natal Rahu, and Mercury is almost the same degree in the USA's 8th house. This indicates a cover up by the USA government with deep secrets because of the 8th house.

Catastrophic Events Rahu in Taurus and Ketu in Scorpio

- Texas City disaster, ship explosion in Texas City, April 16, 1947, killed 581 people.
- Sri Lankan civil war civil war between government and Tamil insurgents, July 23, 1983, killed 80,000-100,000 people.
- Bhopal gas tragedy, chemical leak killed thousands in Bhopal, India, December three, 1984, killed 15,000-20,000 people.
- Typhoon Vamco, typhoon affected the Philippines and Vietnam, November 11, 2020, killed 102 people.

Predictions for April 07, 2039 to December 09, 2040 – Rahu in Taurus and Ketu in Scorpio

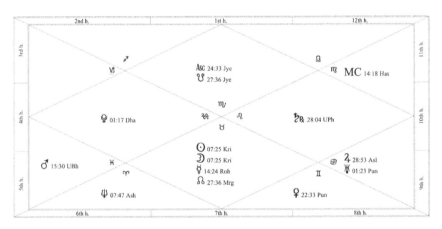

Transiting Jupiter will enter into Cancer March 3, 2039, and remain there until June 1, 2039. This is another indication of a great healing as Jupiter's most powerful position is in Cancer, which is its exaltation sign. This also indicates a spiritual revolution and transformation that is occurring globally on earth.

October 22, 2038, Saturn enters Virgo, but on April 5, 2039, Saturn enters back into Leo. Saturn will enter Virgo July 12, 2039, where it will remain for the next two years. Saturn will prosper in the sign of Virgo as it will help with healing, restructuring, and building new industry in this sign. In 2039 Jupiter will also enter Virgo, but only briefly as it will go back into Leo from April 5, 2039 to June 29, 2040. From June 29, 2040, Jupiter will enter Virgo where it will remain there for the rest of the year and all of 2040.

Jupiter will conjunct Saturn October 31, 2040, in Virgo at 23°. This Jupiter Saturn conjunction occurs every 20 years and always seems to fall in the beginning of the year that begins every two decades, 1920, 1940, 1960, 1980, 2000, 2020, 2040. The Jupiter Saturn conjunction usually pertains to growth expansion and major changes with the economy.

Another rare transformational event is that Pluto will transit into the sign of Aquarius initially March 5, 2039, but will revert back to Capricorn August 23, 2039. By January 15, 2040, Pluto will enter and stay in Aquarius. As Pluto transits through the sign of Aquarius for the next 20 years it will promote major transformational changes for humanity and change how governments are run. There will be more focus on ecology and healing the planet as well as discoveries in healing and health.

2nd h.		3rd h.	4th h.		5th h.	
	♓	♈		♉		♊
		♅℞ 06:35 Ash	☊ 18:35 Roh		♂℞ 24:00 Pun	
1st h. ASC 11:09 Sat	♒	December Solar Eclipse 39 Thu 12-15-2039 11:31:46 Washington, District of Columbia USA Timezone: 5 DST: 0 Latitude: 38N53'42 Longitude: 77W02'11 Ayanamsha : -24:24:38 Lahiri			♆℞ 08:25 Pus	♋ 6th h.
12th h. ♀ 29:18 Dha	♑					♌ 7th h.
	♐	♍	♎		♍	
		☉17:52 Jye ☿18:35 Jye ☋24:34 Jye ☌29:08 Jye	♀ 19:33 Swa		♃ 05:51 UPh ♄ 16:26 Has	
11th h.		10th h.	9th h.		8th h.	

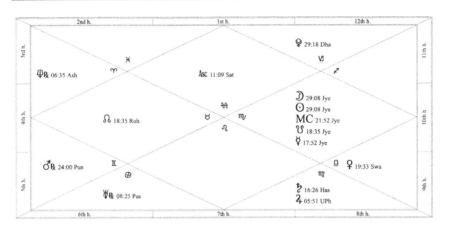

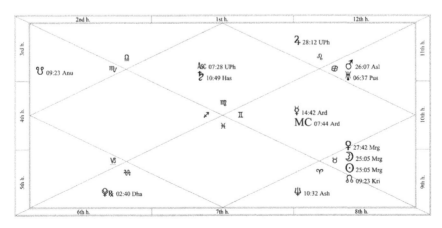

The year of 2040 marks a new era in healing as well as a new way of working with governments and an enormous change with how currency and money are exchanged. The space age is upon us and our connections to space stations and aliens will not be unknown or a mystery anymore. We will be working with aliens by this time as the 2038-2039 crises may mean aliens need to intervene.

There seems to be a higher intelligence and an evolution of consciousness during this time. There will be many discoveries in longevity and an understanding of healing and the human body.

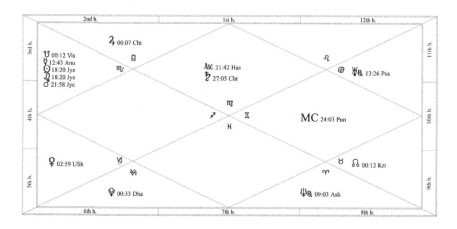

CHAPTER 13

Rahu in Aries and Ketu in Libra

December 09, 2040 to June 21, 2042

There were major disasters concerning tsunamis and earthquakes as well as problems with machinery such as in the Challenger space shuttle and nuclear disasters with a power plant in Russia. Rahu can be extremely intense in Aries especially in the nakshatra Ashwini as it's ruled by Ketu. These points seem to also affect the economy, so these are the things we're going to be looking for in the following period of 2041.

Nakshatras Activated

Rahu in Aries (Ashwini, Bharani, Krittika) and Ketu in Libra (Chitra, Swati, Vishaka).

What happened before:

The cardinal signs Aries and Libra are powerful action-oriented signs that produce big events. The fire and air elements of Aries and Libra are instigators that constitute new beginnings. Progressive thinking and problem solving are the result of events that transpire while Rahu and Ketu create eclipses here. Some events can be dangerous with the level of brash and impulsive energy that comes with this territory.

The nakshatra Bharani can instigate great obstacles to overcome and through persistence, brings breakthroughs and breakdowns in global affairs. The 1929 stock market crash occurred while Rahu was in Aries and Ketu in Libra. This was the beginning of the Great Depression.

Rahu was in Aries and Ketu in Libra when a devastating tsunami hit Malaysia at the very end of 2004. The Indian Ocean earthquake occurred on December 26, 2004, with the epicenter off the west coast of Sumatra, Indonesia. The shock had a magnitude of 9.1–9.3. An estimated 228,000 people died. This quake affected many other countries as well such as Indonesia, Sri Lank, India, Maldives, and Thailand.

The nakshatra Swati is ruled by Rahu and can have devastating effects. The nakshatra Ashwini is ruled by Ketu, compounding the effects of Rahu and Ketu. The stock market crash had Ketu in Swati. The tsunami of Malaysia had Rahu in Ashwini.

2nd h. 27	3rd h. 30	4th h. 27	5th h. 29
⛢℞ 16:34 UBh	☊ 19:39 Bha	♃ 23:30 Mrg	♀ 26:40 Pun
1st h. 32 ASC 11:43 Sat	Stock Market Crash Tue 10-01-1929 16:15:43 New York, New York USA		**6th h. 41**
12th h. 23	Timezone: 5 DST: 0 Latitude: 40N42'51 Longitude: 74W00'22 Ayanamsha : -22:52:21 Lahiri	♅ 09:35 Mag ♀ 14:39 PPh	**7th h. 22**
♄ 01:56 Mul	♂ 03:59 Cht ☋ 19:39 Swa	☽ 01:59 UPh ☉ 15:19 Has ☿℞ 28:13 Cht	
11th h. 28	10th h. 30	9th h. 26	8th h. 22

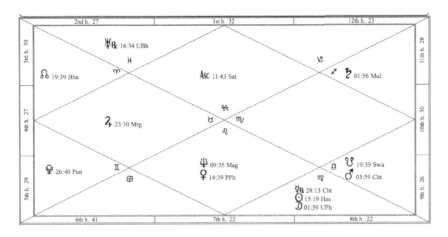

Malaysian Tsunami
Sun 12-26-2004
00:30:00
Sumahit, Sabah
Malaysia
Timezone: -8 DST: 0
Latitude: 04N27'00
Longitude: 116E02'00
Ayanamsha : -23:55:28 Lahiri

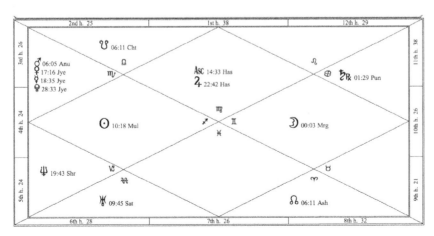

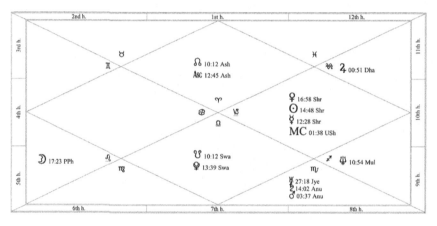

On January 28, 1986, the Space Shuttle Challenger broke apart 73 seconds after takeoff and into its flight, killing all seven crew members on board, while the world watched it unfold on television. The spacecraft disintegrated 46,000 feet (14 km) above the Atlantic Ocean, off the coast of Cape Canaveral, Florida, at 11:39 a.m. EST (16:39 UTC). It was the first fatal accident involving an American spacecraft while in flight.

In 1892 Thomas Edison and his personal assistant Samuel Insull changed the electrical industry forever by setting up electrical stations in major cities. During this time Uranus, which is the planet that rules electricity was conjunct Ketu in Libra indicating a major change and awakening in this discovery. Ketu conjunct a planet brings us into another world. The world was rapidly changing at this time as one of the most significant conjunctions was also occurring at this time, the Pluto and Neptune conjunction. This rare conjunction only happens about 493 years. So, it was in the late 1800s that this occurred and with it the world transformed remarkably with consciousness and discoveries. This was the time of the Spiritualist Movement, where a new wave of consciousness came into the world with mystics like Emerson, Thoreau, and Madam Blavatsky. Spiritualists believed that spirits of the dead could communicate with the living and that spirits were more advanced than humans. Many participated in séances, including President Lincoln in the White House.

Humanity was transformed and began an entirely different mindset. Humans could not conceive of the ideas that came about at this time in previous years. This is exactly what the cycles of the outer planets produce, which is a change in consciousness. This is another example how the cycles of the lunar nodes activate the timing. This came about with Ketu together with Uranus at this specific time. When Rahu is in Aries this means a new beginning because Aries is the sign of birth and new beginnings.

2nd h.	3rd h.	4th h.	5th h.
♓	♈	♉	♊
♃℞ 22:52 Rev	☊ 15:15 Bha	♀℞ 16:31 Roh ♅℞ 17:39 Roh	
♒	Electricity for All		♋
♂ 18:25 Sat ☽ 17:00 Sat Asc 00:55 Dha	Sun 11-27-1892 12:00:00 West Orange, New Jersey		
♑	USA Timezone: 5 DST: 0		♌
	Latitude: 40N47'55 Longitude: 74W14'21 Ayanamsha : -22:21:30 Lahiri		
♐	♏	♎	♍
☿ 04:40 Mul	☉ 13:36 Anu MC 17:08 Jye	♀ 06:48 Swa ☋ 15:15 Swa ♇ 15:50 Swa	♄ 17:55 Has
11th h.	10th h.	9th h.	8th h.

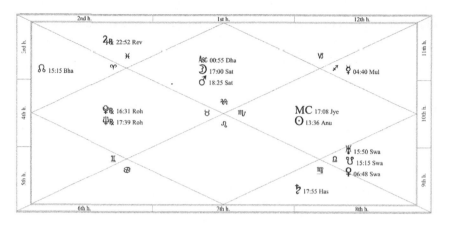

Catastrophic Events Rahu in Aries and Ketu in Libra

- Nigerian civil war, conflict in Nigeria over succession of Biafra, July 6, 1967, killed 1 to 3 million people.
- Chernobyl nuclear disaster, explosion at Chernobyl nuclear power plant, April 26, 1986, killed 4,000 plus people.
- Iran earthquake, Quake in Iran, December 26, 2003, killed 26,000 people.
- USA war in Iraq, invasion of Iraq by USA forces, March 20, 2003, killed 200,000 people.
- Indian Ocean earthquake and tsunami, earthquake and tsunami in Southeast Asia, December 26, 2004, killed 230,000-280,000 people.

Predictions for December 17, 2040 – June 21, 2042 – Rahu in Aries and Ketu in Libra

11th h.		12th h.		1st h.		2nd h.	
♂ 15:32 UBh ♀ 03:45 UBh	♓	♅ 11:17 Ash ☽ 16:04 Bha ☉ 16:04 Bha ☋ 20:50 Bha	♈	☿ 02:37 Kri ASC 14:15 Roh	♉		♊
♆ 03:56 Dha	♒		April Solar Eclipse 41 Tue 04-30-2041 07:45:46 Washington, District of Columbia USA Timezone: 5 DST: 1 Latitude: 38N53'42 Longitude: 77W02'11 Ayanamsha : -24:25:50 Lahiri			♇ 09:41 Pus	♋
MC 21:18 Shr	♑						♌
	♐		♏		♎	2 ℞ 00:41 Cht ☋ 20:50 Vis	♄ ℞ 25:12 Cht
8th h.		7th h.		6th h.		5th h.	

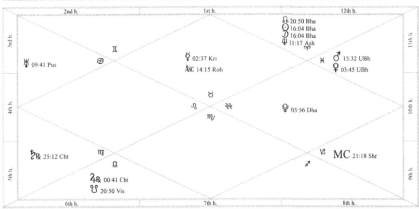

10th h.		11th h.		12th h.		1st h.	
	♓	☋ 11:41 Ash ♇ ℞ 12:23 Ash	♈		♉	ASC 05:24 Mrg	♊
MC 13:14 Sat ♀ ℞ 01:51 Dha	♒		October Solar Eclipse 41 Thu 10-24-2041 21:30:19 Washington, District of Columbia USA Timezone: 5 DST: 1 Latitude: 38N53'42 Longitude: 77W02'11 Ayanamsha : -24:26:17 Lahiri			♂ 14:08 Pus ♅ 18:03 Asl	♋
	♑						♌
	♐		♏	♇ 03:28 Cht ☉ 07:34 Swa ☽ 07:31 Swa ↋ 15:32 Swa	♎	☿ 20:18 Has ♀ 20:48 Has	♍
7th h.		6th h.		5th h.		4th h.	

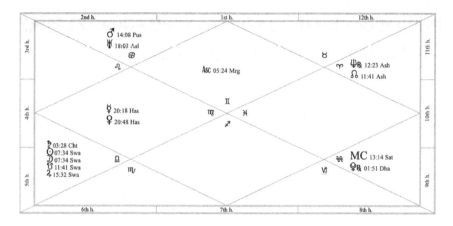

A new consciousness arrives in 2040 through 2041 as Pluto transits through Aquarius for the next 20 years. This transit will bring a major change and transformation with massive healing. There will be discoveries for mental disorders and diseases such as addictions, depression, and the chemistry of the brain. Even strides in advancing intelligence and opening and expanding the mind will be discovered. This is a new era for healing of suffering from disease as well as banishing hunger throughout the planet. We are on our way to a spiritual evolution that changes the course and direction of humanity. There will be a much higher understanding, appreciation, and respect for the spiritual arts, especially the Divine science of them all – astrology!

Conclusion

I felt the need to write this book as one of my legacies to help the world understand the power and the purpose of the most Divine science of all – Astrology. When you understand the connections of Rahu and Ketu as our destiny, where Rahu brings us into the world and Ketu takes us out of this world, you begin to understand the workings of the Universe. The nodal axis connects us to our future and our past and determines the evolution of humanity. Humanity's evolution continues through world events. The outer planets Uranus, Neptune and Pluto rule the collective unconscious of humanity and direct our level of understanding. It is when these planets evolve through certain signs and form aspects to each other that our level of conscious evolves to higher levels.

Mars is the planet that triggers the events. This gives us the timing of when the events will occur. As Rahu and Ketu are in a sign for 18 months, they can be conjunct the outer planets for very long periods of time, but as soon as Mars transits near Rahu or Ketu it is the trigger to activate these longstanding conjunctions and oppositions. This is the activation that causes the timing of these enormous changes.

It is my soul desire to help others understand the cycles of humanity due to the planets and the transits of Rahu and Ketu. This allows us to gain clarity in our own personal lives and gain an understanding of the signs that create the most catastrophic events on planet Earth. I felt the need to write this book and make this prediction in my lifetime, in an effort to help humanity prepare and possibly even avert such difficulties. It is possible that with the trends of consciousness on the planet these events may need to occur for the evolution and transformational changes of humanity.

Following the timeframes of when Rahu is in Gemini and Ketu is in Sagittarius the planet will go through a healing because this will trigger the start of a wakeup call after a crisis.

This healing will occur in 2038 to 2039 when Rahu will be in Taurus and Ketu in Scorpio because they are in their exaltation signs, indicating a revival after the destruction. Humanity will awaken to another level of consciousness. It is my hope and my dream that I will still be alive during these times to be able to see how life evolves, and watch humanity awaken to a higher level of consciousness. My greatest wish is for people to respect and value the power and healing that the knowledge of astrology can bestow upon humankind.

As we move towards the age of Aquarius it is my hope that the science of astrology expands and goes deeper becoming a part of every person's life. I have always said that we are only on the tip of the iceberg to understanding the power and the uses of astrology. Astrology has given me the clarity and a new understanding of the power held by the divine through the movements of the stars and planets. It is how they are connected, which we call sacred geometry, that highlights our growth and development of cosmic consciousness.

We are the cosmic consciousness and as we discover who we really are through the understanding of the stars and the planets, we will transform to a higher level of understanding realizing we are one with each other and the universe.

Signed
Joni Patry

List of Charts

Joni's Recent Predictions
BEFORE
They Happened!

Trump's Presidential win 2024

Trump Assassination Attempt (2024)

President Trump would get the Coronavirus (2020)

Coronavirus (2019)

Bitcoin (2017)

New French President (2017)

Trump's Presidential win (2016)

Turkish Coup (2016)

Secrets and Scandals on the Clintons (2016)

Coupe in Istanbul, Turkey (2016)

Attack in Paris (2015)

Air Disaster with Malaysian Airlines (2014)

Attack in Egypt (2013)

Protest in Istanbul (2013)

Earthquake in Japan (2011)

Joni Patry's Products and Services

www.galacticcenter.org

GALACTIC PLANNER

www.galacticplanner.com

Your Personal Astrology planner in your personal calendar with daily accurate customized predictions just for you

Learn Vedic Astrology with Joni Patry and become certified

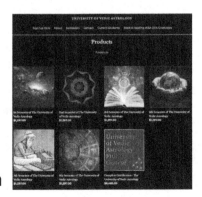

www.universityofvedicastrology.com

JONI PATRY
WELCOME TO MY PATREON!

www.patreon.com/c/JoniPatry/posts

Joni Patry

Exclusive & uncensored videos & personal "ask your astrologer" opportunities

Joni Patry's Astrology insights Magazine

www.astrologyinsightsmagazine.com

JONI PATRY'S ASTROLOGY INSIGHTS MAGAZINE

Schedule a one on one reading with Joni Patry

www.galacticcenter.org/consultations

 @JoniPatryVedicAstrologer

 @JoniPatry

 JoniPatryVedicAstrologer

 joni_patry

 @JoniPatry

Other Books by Joni Patry

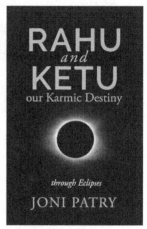

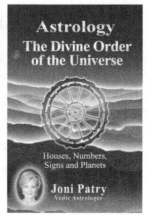

www.galacticcenter.org/books

Available on
amazon.com

Made in the USA
Coppell, TX
16 April 2025

48391030R00105